The Critical Idiom

Founder Editor: John D. Jump (1969–1976)

13 Irony and the Ironic

Irony and the Ironic

D. C. Muecke

Methuen

London and New York

First published in 1970
by Methuen & Co. Ltd
11 New Fetter Lane, London EC4P 4EE

Published in the USA by
Methuen & Co.
in association with Methuen, Inc.
733 Third Avenue, New York, NY 10017
Second edition 1982

© 1970 and 1982 D. C. Muecke

Typeset by Scarborough Typesetting Services
and printed in Great Britain by
J. W. Arrowsmith Ltd, Bristol

British Library Cataloguing in Publication Data

Muecke, D. C.
Irony and the ironic.—(The Critical
idiom; 13)
1. Irony in literature
I. Title   II. Series

ISBN 0 416 32940 3
ISBN 0 416 32860 1 (Pbk)

Library of Congress Cataloging in Publication Data

Muecke, D. C. (Douglas Colin)
Irony and the ironic.
(The Critical idiom; 13)
Second ed. of: Irony. 1970.
Bibliography: p.
Includes index.
1. Irony.   2. Irony in literature.
I. Title.   II. Series.
BH301.I7M8   1982   809′.91   81-22294

ISBN 0 416 32940 3   AACR2
ISBN 0 416 32860 1 (Pbk)

Contents

To
Barbara Wall

fellow student

Preface to the second edition

The change of title is designed solely to mark the fact that, with the exceptions of the section entitled 'Early concepts of irony' and a few paragraphs here and there, the present work constitutes less a revision of my earlier work in this series than a complete rewriting.

D.C.M.

Acknowledgements

The author would like to thank Professor Leslie Bodi of Monash University for what has been more than twenty years of friendly and helpful ironological consociation.

The author and publishers would like to thank the following for permission to reproduce copyright material:

Martin Esslin and *Encounter* for 'The Solution' (Bertolt Brecht, trans. Martin Esslin, June 1959).

1
Introduction

Orientation

'When all else fails, read the directions.' These words, printed on a can of paint, show that irony plays a part in everyday living, a relatively small part, perhaps, though many other instances could be cited. Such 'folk irony' generally offers no great challenge; something more sly or covert like 'The directions may be ignored' might only have proved puzzling, though the message is much the same. In this work, more attention will be paid to irony in literature than to the simpler ironies practised or observed in life at large. Not that a sociological approach to irony need be uninteresting: one would like to know what parts both Verbal Irony and the shared recognition of ironical situations and happenings play in the daily life of different social groupings, and whether people are more likely or less likely to be ironical, more alert or less alert to irony, according to social class and status, degree of urbanization, strength of religious or political convictions, occupation, sex, education, IQ rating or personality type. The hero of Svevo's *Confessions of Zeno* remarks that 'Accountants are by nature a race of animals much inclined to irony.' Since, however, Svevo, not to mention his hero, had had a career in commerce, the statement if true may be ironical — but if ironical may be true.

'I had long been hearing, in the English colony at Tokyo, that no Japanese can understand irony (whereas the Chinese, of course, use it all the time).' So William Empson, who taught in both Japanese and Chinese universities in the 1930s (*New York Review of Books*, 12 June 1975, p. 37). On the other hand, a desultory reading in anthologies of Chinese and Japanese classics (admittedly in English translations) might easily give a contrary impression: that the Chinese are straightforward and practical with a robust sense of humour, that the Japanese are involuted, introspective and sophisticated. The way in which the *tanka* was used in the tenth-century *Kagerō Nikki*, for example, for politely conveying reproach or disagreement through the indirectness of metaphor and innuendo, seems very close to irony, but obviously only someone at home in both Japanese and Western culture could say how close. The *Goncourt Journal* (20 March 1884) infers from the conversation of a single Japanese visitor that 'les Japonais ont une aimable ironie, une ironie un peu à la française'. In his *Wax and Gold: Tradition and Innovation in Ethiopian Culture* (Chicago, 1965), Donald Levine tells us of the Amharic people who practise a form of verse not unlike the *tanka*, in that it has a literal and a hidden meaning often at odds with one another. And the more one comes to know of oral cultures, the more one is inclined to suspect that irony, or something like it, is a widespread phenomenon, though only the co-operation of many could provide what would nevertheless be desirable, a global survey showing which cultures practise irony, or something like it, most extensively, intensively and variously, which are most alert to ironic situations and events, and which have independently evolved concepts of irony.

This work draws only upon Western culture – from Moscow to Melbourne, via Madrid and Manhattan – and even then much is excluded. Specifically it excludes any detailed considerations of irony in the non-verbal arts, partly because of the expense of illustration, partly for want of expertise, and partly – this will perhaps confirm the lack of expertise – on the grounds that there seem to be no ways of being ironical that are specific to music, painting, landscape gardening, kinetic art, patisserie and so on. Non-representative art can be ironical in perhaps only two ways: incongruities of formal properties and parodies of the clichés, mannerisms, styles, conventions, ideologies and theories of earlier artists, schools or periods: 'The hedgehog collection of solar panels on the roof makes mockery of the seriousness with which some diehard low-energy architects treat these symbols of our new energy source' (*The* [Melbourne] *Age*). The musical parodies described in Thomas Mann's *Doctor Faustus* are more complex than this, but it is the programmatic nature of much of the music that makes the greater complexity possible. As for representative art, the ironic painter, who paints his own studio with himself in it painting a self-portrait is not in principle different from the novelist whose novel is about himself writing an autobiographical novel. Or imagine this ironic picture: the subject, a religious hypocrite, is placed in an attitude of devotion; on one wall hangs a Magdalen that manages to be both pious and pornographic; and opposite, so placed within the window curtains (of penitential purple) as to suggest it has been overlooked or forgotten, is a lady's garter. But could this, however well done, achieve as much as Molière does in the speeches he gives Tartuffe?

What irony is and how it works; what it's for and what it's worth; what it's made from and how it's made up; how we know it when we see it; where the concept came from and where it's going: these questions and some others it will be the endeavour of this work to answer, at greater or lesser length and within the limitations already indicated.

The ironical and the non-ironical

The importance of irony in literature is beyond question. One need not accept the view, put forward at least twice on different grounds, that all art, or all literature, is essentially ironic – or the view that all good literature must be ironic. One need only list the major writers in whose work irony is significantly present: Homer, Aeschylus, Sophocles, Euripides, Aristophanes, Thucydides, Plato, Cicero, Horace, Catullus, Juvenal, Tacitus, Lucian, Boccaccio, Chaucer, Villon, Ariosto, Shakespeare, Cervantes, Pascal, Molière, Racine, Swift, Pope, Voltaire, Johnson, Gibbon,

Diderot, Goethe, Stendhal, Jane Austen, Byron, Heine, Baudelaire, Gogol, Dostoevsky, Flaubert, Ibsen, Tolstoy, Mark Twain, Henry James, Chekhov, Shaw, Pirandello, Proust, Thomas Mann, Kafka, Musil and Brecht. What comparable list could be drawn up of writers whose work is not ironical at all or only occasionally, minimally or doubtfully ironical? Such a list implies the impossibility of separating an interest in irony as an art from an interest in great literature; one leads directly to the other.

The importance of being ironical, however, cannot be established without at the same time establishing the importance of being earnest. The golden eggs of irony could not be laid so abundantly if we were not knee-deep in geese. As scepticism presupposes credulity, so irony needs 'alazony', which is Greek for braggartism but in works on irony is shorthand for any form of self-assurance or naïvety. To say that history is the record of human fallibility and that the history of thought is the record of the recurrent discovery that what we assured ourselves was the truth, was in truth only a seeming truth is to say that literature has always had an endless field in which to observe and practise irony. This suggests that irony has basically a corrective function. It is like a gyroscope that keeps life on an even keel or straight course, restoring the balance when life is being taken too seriously or, as some tragedies show, not seriously enough, stabilizing the unstable but also destabilizing the excessively stable. Or we might think of it as a *sine qua non* of life and repeat what Thomas Mann quotes Goethe as saying, 'Irony is that little grain of salt that alone renders the dish palatable', or agree with Kierkegaard that 'as philosophers claim that no true philosophy is possible without doubt, so by the same token one may claim that no authentic human life is possible without irony' (*The Concept of Irony*, trans. Lee M. Capel, 1966, p. 338).

This should not be taken as advocating an ironic presence in every work of art, still less in all human behaviour, where in any case it would not be possible, since, as noted, eggs need geese. Moreover, the non-ironic is not necessarily alazonic; that is to say, there are occasions in life and art, let us hope, when irony is not called for. We can say this without accepting Kierkegaard's firm subordination of the ironic to the ethic sphere: when Goethe in Italy offered himself a gorgeous Italian peach did he always add a '*Körnchen Salz*'?

What then are these occasions from which we would hope to exclude irony, if only to preserve some variety in life and art? In 1945 Auden wrote:

> Can I learn to suffer
> Without saying something ironic or funny
> On suffering?

('The Sea and the Mirror')

I expect in the end he did learn. I expect life can be relied upon to provide everyone with crises of passion from which irony retreats, in which there is no room for reflection, detachment or balance. Art too can be single-minded, that is, unironic; and if this is more likely to be true of the non-verbal arts it might be explained by the difference of the media. The non-verbal arts – music, dance, architecture, for example – appeal in the first instance to and through the senses. Literature, with language as its medium, is inescapably ideational. Of course we must qualify such bald statements. The informed gallery visitor or concert-goer knows how much in a still life or a sonata may be art or music criticism and therefore may be ironic. Conversely, language has its phonetic or sensuous element that in literature becomes 'music' and may, therefore, be single-minded. Nevertheless, the distinction remains, and it is precisely the exceptions and the qualifications that prove the rule. For it is when literature is most musical, in lyric poetry, that it is, by and large, least ironical. And it is when a painting is 'intellectual' or 'literary', whether in 'making a statement' or 'conveying a message', that it can be ironic. But when it is intent upon formal perfection or technical innovation or absolute expression, then irony may be felt as distracting or intrusive.

Art then is acceptably non-ironic when the appeal is simplest, most immediate and most absorbing, whether by approaching the aesthetic opacity of pure sensuousness or pure form, or by approaching the aesthetic transparency of the purely sublime, where intensity of feeling carries us swiftly through and beyond all consciousness of the medium. Combined, these two ways are summed up in what Milton says of poetry, that it is, compared with rhetoric, 'more simple, sensuous and passionate'.

The non-ironic, therefore, need not be restricted to what the ironic corrects or redeems or authenticates. We may agree with Anatole France in his essay on Rabelais that 'the world without irony would be like a forest without birds' but we need not wish every tree more bird than leaf. We might instead see the ironic and the non-ironic as, in part, complementary opposites, as reason and emotion are, each desirable and necessary but neither sufficient for all our needs. Thomas Mann, in the following, went some way towards this view:

> Irony and radicalism – this is an alternative and an Either-Or. An intelligent man has the choice (*if* he has it) to be either ironical or radical. There is, in all decency, no third possibility. Which he is depends on the argument that he accepts as ultimately and absolutely valid: life or spirit. . . . For the radical man life is no argument. *Fiat spiritus, pereat vita!* But the words of irony are: 'Can truth be an argument if it is a matter of life?'
>
> (*Meditations of a Non-Political Man*, quoted from Erich Heller, *The Ironic German*, London, 1958, pp. 236–7)

The 'third possibility' is the impossible but none the less obligatory (hence ironical!) injunction to be both ironical *and* radical. Thomas Mann was later to say, 'Irony always aims at both sides, at life as well as at the spirit' (ibid.). But this, as we shall see, implies a higher irony, definable as a serene, detached acceptance of the eternal opposition of life and spirit, the ironical (in a more sceptical sense) and the radical.

Getting to grips with irony

'Only that which has no history can be defined' (Nietzsche). For this and other reasons the concept of irony is vague, unstable and multiform. The word 'irony' does not now mean only what it meant in earlier centuries, it does not mean in one country all it may mean in another, nor in the street what it may mean in the study, nor to one scholar what it may mean to another. The different phenomena the word is applied to may seem very tenuously related. The semantic evolution of the word has been haphazard; historically, our concept of irony is the cumulative result of our having, from time to time over the centuries, applied the term sometimes intuitively, sometimes heedlessly, sometimes deliberately, to such phenomena as seemed, perhaps mistakenly, to bear a sufficient resemblance to certain other phenomena to which we had already been applying the term. So the concept of irony at any one time may be likened to a ship at anchor when both wind and current, variable and constant forces, are dragging it slowly from its anchorage. It is only very recently that the word has achieved full colloquial status, together with a certain modishness that has led 'How ironical!' to oust 'What a coincidence!' and even 'How odd!' Example: 'The irony of the dismissal [of Gooch by Hughes for 99 in the Third Test] was that Hughes was dismissed for 99 in the first Test' (*The Australian*, 2–3 February 1980).

There is little to be done about this. Most people will continue to use a word like 'irony' without knowing or caring to know precisely how it has been used before or whether there is not a more suitable word already in use. As for ironologists, they will convince themselves very easily that any proposed restriction or extension of the meaning of the word, their own excepted, must be ruled out. So A. R. Thompson (*The Dry Mock*, 1948, p. 15) will argue in vain that irony is only irony when the effect is one of mingled pain and amusement; Guido Almansi (*L'Ironie de l'ironie*, Centro Internazionale di Semiotica e di Linguistica, Urbino,

1979) that the truly ironic is the ambiguously ironic; and Empson (op. cit.) that the 'basic situation for the trope of irony' is what, forty odd years ago, 'everyone assumed' it to be — A, speaking ironically, is correctly understood, as intended, by B but misunderstood, as intended, by C, a 'censor' or 'stupid tyrant'. Empson admits his 'pure form' of irony is seldom found, but seems, like the others, willing to deprive us of a word for the more frequently occurring phenomena that his definition excludes. When Cleanth Brooks (*The Well-Wrought Urn*, 1949, p. 191) wishes to extend the semantic range of the word 'irony' on the grounds that it is 'the most general term that we have for the kind of qualification which the various elements in a context receive from the context' he seems content to leave us without words to distinguish between the irony (in his new sense) of Tennyson's 'Tears, Idle Tears' and the irony (in an older sense) of Eliot's 'The Love Song of J. Alfred Prufrock'.

In the matter of definition then, I shall not insist (except when I forget) that everyone set his watch by mine. I shall say what the time is according to me, since that is the only time I can be sure of. My attempts at definition and analysis beginning in the next chapter will, however, be prefaced by a sketch of the history of the concept of irony so that the reader can check his own watch.

Here, in the meantime, is a set of examples illustrating something of the range of what I expect most people with an 'English' literary education would regard as irony. The names are descriptive or conventional; no taxonomic aspiration should be inferred. The reader is invited to identify what the examples may have in common.

1   *Irony as rhetorical enforcement*

The Government has made small slips before, of course. It has made minor errors of economic policy. It has occasionally deported the wrong people. It has gambled on the wrong defence system. It invaded the wrong country. All these peccadilloes could be forgiven. . . . But now a member of the Government has *slept with the wrong woman*, and as a consequence severely strained this country's newsprint resources.

(Michael Frayn, commenting on the Profumo case,
The Observer, 1963)

2 *Mock-modesty or Self-disparaging Irony*

Also I prey you to foryeve it me,
Al have I nat set folk in hir degree
Here in this tale, as that they sholde stonde.
My wit is short, ye may wel understonde.

(Chaucer, *The Canterbury Tales*)

3 *Ironic Mockery*

All I know is that the book is gone, and I feel as Wordsworth is generally supposed to have felt when he became aware that Lucy was in her grave, and exclaimed so emphatically that this would make a considerable difference to him, or words to that effect. . . . Lucy was not particularly attractive – no more was Frost's *Lives of Eminent Christians*; there were few to praise her, and of those few, still fewer could bring themselves to like her.

(Samuel Butler, 'Quis desiderio . . .?')

4 *Irony by analogy*

The Beggar's Opera, *Animal Farm*.

5 *Non-verbal Irony*

The kings of Siam, it is said, had a way of punishing nobles by honouring them with a gift of a sacred white elephant, a gift they were unable to decline but obliged to maintain at ruinous expense.

6 *Ironic Naïvety*

> The golf links lie so near the mill
> > That almost every day
> The laboring children can look out
> > And see the men at play.
>
> (Sarah N. Cleghorn, 'The Golf Links Lie So Near The Mill')

7 *Dramatic Irony, or the spectacle of blindness*

HASTINGS.   Ere a fortnight make me elder,
            I'll send some packing, that yet think not on it.
CATESBY.   'Tis a vile thing to die, my gracious lord,
            When men are unprepar'd and look not for it.
HASTINGS.   O monstrous, monstrous! and so falls it out
            With Rivers, Vaughan, Grey, and so 'twill do
            With some men else, who think themselves as safe
            As thou and I, who, as thou know'st, are dear
            To princely Richard, and to Buckingham.
CATESBY.   The princes both make high account of you;
            (*aside*) For they account his head upon the bridge.
                              (*King Richard III*, III, ii, 62–72)

8 *Unconscious Irony* (Samuel Butler's term)

B____, Francis William. On July 19th, at Caulfield Hospital, loved husband of Rita, beloved father of Len, Margaret (Mrs Jenkins), Rev. Fr Bill, Peter, Jim, Rosemary (Mrs Forster) and Tim, fond father-in-law of Nona, Alan, Monica, Lorraine, Paul and Kate, loved grandfather of 41 grandchildren and 2 great-grandchildren.
                    Rest in Peace.

                                              (Death notice)

9 *Self-betraying Irony*

'They ought to be treated just like they did Willie and them.

Worse. I wish I could round up some people and kill those men myself.'

'That ain't no Christian way to talk,' Portia said. 'Us can just rest back and know they going to be chopped up with pitch-forks and fried everlasting by Satan.'

(Carson McCullers, *The Heart is a Lonely Hunter*, London, 1954, p. 203)

10 *Irony of Events*

(a) 'Nothing odd will do long. *Tristram Shandy* did not last.'

(Dr Johnson)

(b) The Romans think they have got rid of an enemy when they banish Coriolanus. But the effect is to drive him into the arms of their traditional enemies, the Volscians, at the head of whose army he returns intending the destruction of Rome.

11 *Cosmic Irony*

The tears that lie about this plightful scene
Of heavy travail in a suffering soul,
Mocked with the forms and feints of royalty
While scarified by briery Circumstance,
Might drive Compassion past her patiency
To hold that some mean, monstrous ironist
Had built this mistimed fabric of the Spheres
To watch the throbbings of its captive lives,
(The which may Truth forfend), and not thy said
Unmaliced, unimpassioned, nescient Will!

(Hardy, *The Dynasts*, Part 2, VI, v)

12 *Ironic Incongruity*

(a) 'Quelle ironie sanglante qu'un palais en face d'une cabane!'

(Théophile Gautier)

(b) 'The archetype of the incongruously ironic is Christ, the perfectly innocent victim excluded from human society.'

(Northrop Frye, *Anatomy of Criticism*, 1957, p. 42)

13 *Double Irony*

There is always a slight cast of irony in the grave, calm, respectful attention impartially bestowed by an intelligent judge on two contending parties, who are pleading their causes before him with all the earnestness of deep conviction, and of excited feeling. What makes the contrast interesting is, that the right and the truth lie on neither side exclusively: that there is no fraudulent purpose, no gross imbecility of intellect, on either: but both have plausible claims and specious reasons to alledge, though each is too much blinded by prejudice or passion to do justice to the views of his adversary. For here the irony lies not in the demeanor of the judge, but is deeply seated in the case itself, which seems to favour each of the litigants, but really eludes them both. And this too it is that lends the highest degree of interest to the conflicts of religious and political parties.

(Connop Thirlwall, 'On the Irony of Sophocles',
Philological Museum, Vol. II, 1833, pp. 489–90)

14 *Catch 22 Irony*

(a) 'There is a terrible irony in the theatre. You're portraying people, ordinary people, but the more you work, the less you're in contact with people outside the theatre.'

(An actress)

(b) Si jeunesse savoit; si vieillesse pouvoit.

(Henri Estienne, *Les Prémices*, Epigramme cxci)

15 *Romantic Irony*

(a) Thomas Mann's *Doctor Faustus*.

(b) – Who's that you were talking to up on the knoll?
   – Some clown who wandered into this [comic] strip by mistake.
   – Good.
   – Why good?
   – If there's a way in, there's a way out.
      (T. K. Ryan, 'Tumbleweeds', a comic strip in *The Age*)

These examples offer a way into the complexities of discourse about irony. The somewhat labyrinthine history of the concept that follows will lead eventually to a sighting of this double-natured quasi-mythological beast as it now exists – double-natured because it is generally accepted that there are two basic forms of irony, different but related and not easily separable, and quasi-mythological because 'irony' is only a concept, one element in a conceptual system which in turn is only a temporarily agreed upon device for making sense of the world. A change at one point in the system (and such a change may already have occurred) could eventually lead to the discovery that the concept of irony as now understood actually prevents us from looking at literature in a new way: it is not inconceivable that 'irony', now a key concept in literary criticism, will follow into limbo the concept of 'sublimity', so indispensable to earlier centuries.

2
The evolution of a concept

Early concepts of irony

There are certain situations and utterances which we do not hesitate to call ironic. Odysseus returns to Ithaca and, sitting disguised as a beggar in his own palace, hears one of the suitors scouting the idea that he (Odysseus) could ever come home again. Later we read (Rieu's translation, but faithful to the sense of the original):

> Odysseus now had the bow in his hands and was twisting it about, testing it this way and that, for fear that the worms might have eaten into the horn in the long absence of its owner. The Suitors glanced at one another and gave vent to some typical comments: 'Ha! Quite the expert, with a critic's eye for bows! No doubt he collects them at home or wants to start a factory, judging by the way he twists it about, just as though he had learnt something useful in his life on the road!'
>
> (*Odyssey*, Book XXI, Penguin Classics)

We can scarcely doubt that the early audiences of the *Odyssey* responded to this situation in much the way we do, feeling that quite distinctive thrill at the spectacle of someone serenely unaware that he is denying the possibility of what has already happened, that *there* before his eyes is the confutation of his words even as he utters them. As for the sarcastic mockery, that too must strike us as having had, nearly three thousand years ago, essentially the same sort of effect as it has today.

I have chosen these two very early examples, one of Situational, one of Verbal Irony – to adopt for the moment a familiar distinction – not to suggest that irony was a Greek invention – I could have cited examples from Exodus and *Beowulf* – but in order first to indicate the antiquity of the phenomenon and then to make the point that irony, both as something we see and respond to and as something we practise, has to be distinguished both from the word 'irony' and the concept of irony. The phenomenon was responded to before it was named and consequently before there could have been a concept of it; and the word existed before it was applied to the phenomenon. If Homer had a word for the suitors' mockery it was neither 'sarkasmos' nor 'eironeia'; the former did not acquire its modern meaning until very late and the latter did not mean Verbal Irony until the time of Aristotle. As for Situational Irony, the irony of the suitors saying in Odysseus' presence that Odysseus would never come home, though it has been the staple irony of drama from Aeschylus to the present day, no one called it irony until the eighteenth century. Nor does it appear that it was ever called anything else, though it is inconceivable that Sophocles and Shakespeare did not clearly recognize the dramatic effect of this kind of irony and certain that Racine did. The word 'irony' appears in some translations of the *Poetics* as a rendering of Aristotle's 'peripeteia' (sudden reversal of circumstances) which perhaps covered part of the meaning of dramatic irony.

Eironeia is first recorded in Plato's *Republic*. Applied to Socrates by one of his victims, it seems to have meant something like 'a smooth, low-down way of taking people in'. For Demosthenes an eiron was one who evaded his responsibilities as a citizen by pretending unfitness. For Theophrastus, an eiron was evasive and non-committal, concealing his enmities, pretending friendship, misrepresenting his acts and never giving a straight answer. Miss Fairfax in *Emma* resembles a Theophrastian eiron in refusing to express her own opinion: 'Was he handsome?' Emma asks, and can get no answer but 'I believe he was reckoned a very fine young man.' This may seem remote from any modern concept of irony, but the reader of Wayne Booth's *Rhetoric of Fiction* (1961) will see how the traditional ironic narrator, a Fielding or an Austen, has evolved, by way of the Flaubertian or Jamesian impersonal ironic narrator, into the narrator who has entirely abandoned any obligation to guide the judgement of his reader, and by so doing has become the modern counterpart of the old Greek *eiron*.

Aristotle, however, possibly because he had Socrates in mind, had rated *eironeia*, in the sense of self-depreciative dissimulation, rather higher than its opposite, 'alazoneia' or boastful dissimulation; modesty, though only pretended, at least seems better than ostentation. At about the same time the word which at first denoted a mode of behaviour came also to be applied to a deceptive use of language; *eironeia* is now a figure in rhetoric: to blame by ironical praise or to praise by ironical blame.

For Cicero, 'ironia' does not have the abusive meanings of the Greek word. In his usage it is either the rhetorical figure or the wholly admirable 'urbane pretence' of a Socrates, irony as a pervasive habit of discourse. When, therefore, we use the word 'irony' of Socrates' way of pretending that he has high hopes of learning from his interlocutor what holiness or justice is, our concept of irony is a Roman one and not a Greek one, though it would be impossible to suppose that Plato was not as appreciative of the quality and effect of his irony as Cicero was. To these two meanings of irony recognized by Cicero, the rhetorician Quintilian added an intermediary one, irony as the elaboration of a figure of speech into an entire argument, the elaboration of some such irony as 'Christianity has its points, after all' into Swift's *Argument [against] the abolishing of Christianity*.

The word 'irony' does not appear in English until 1502 and did not come into general literary use until the early eighteenth century; Dryden, for example, used it only once. English, however, was rich in colloquial terms for verbal usages which we might regard as embryonic irony: fleer, flout, gibe, jeer, mock, scoff, scorn, taunt. Puttenham's *Arte of English Poesie* (ed. G. D. Willcock and A. Walker, London, 1936) actually translates ironia as 'Drie Mock' and this clearly indicates an appreciation of the deadpan quality of a more subtle degree of verbal irony. During the late seventeenth century and the eighteenth century wide use was made of the words 'derision', 'droll', 'rally', 'banter', 'smoke', 'roast', and 'quiz', and these no doubt helped to keep the word 'irony' a literary word. Swift, in the *Journal to Stella* (25 February 1712–13), writes 'Ld Tr[easurer] met me last night at Ld Mashams, & thanked me for my company in a Jear because I had not dind with him in 3 days.'

In England, as in the rest of modern Europe, the concept of irony developed very slowly. The more interesting meanings in Cicero and Quintilian – irony as a way of treating one's opponent in an argument and as the verbal strategy of a whole argument – were ignored at first, and for two hundred years and more irony was regarded principally as a figure of speech. The word was defined as 'saying the contrary of what one means', as 'saying one thing but meaning another', as 'praising in order to blame and blaming in order to praise', and as 'mocking and scoffing'. It was also used to mean dissimulation, even non-ironical dissimulation, understatement, and parody (once at least, by Pope). It was not until the first half of the eighteenth century, the age of *The Bicker-staff Papers, The History of John Bull, The Shortest Way with the Dissenters, The Beggar's Opera, Jonathan Wild* and *The Narrative of Dr Robert Norris, concerning the Strange and Deplorable Frenzy of Mr John Dennis, an Officer of the Custom-House,* that the meaning of the word 'irony' was again extended to include such works as these. A few writers, some with Cicero's discussion of Socrates clearly in their mind, are aware of irony as a mode of behaviour. Shaftesbury is noteworthy for having advised himself to adopt a 'soft irony', an ironic manner outwardly accommodating and amiable (though not devoid of raillery) and inwardly serene and reserved.

By the middle of the eighteenth century the concept of irony in England, and, as far as I know, in other European countries, had scarcely evolved in its broad outlines beyond the point already reached in Quintilian. It is true that one finds 'irony' and 'ironical' being used here and there — for example, Nashe (1589), Burton (1621), Sir Thomas Browne (1646), George Daniel (1649) and Fielding (1730) — in senses that anticipate or seem to anticipate later developments. But even when the word is unmistakably being used in a new way these are isolated usages not taken up by others, or the authors themselves are perhaps not conscious of the new sense they have invented. Fielding is one author who might repay examination as someone not likely to use words inadvisedly. In his *The Temple Beau* (1730) he makes Young Pedant say 'I rejoice in the irony [of being "called coxcomb by a woman"]'. This, though superficially alike, is not the affectionate or teasing irony of dispraising in order to praise but something radically different. Young Pedant explains that the values of women are so topsy-turvy that when they dispraise they may be said to have praised. The woman has not spoken ironically; but it is *as if* she had. This was a radically new expansion of the concept of irony. In 1748 Fielding gave the word another new application, using it of the satiric strategy (as old in practice as the Socratic dialogues and Lucian's *Sale of Lives* and familiar to every play-goer and novel-reader) of inventing or presenting a foolish character who ineptly supports and so unconsciously betrays the view the author wishes to condemn. This 'Self-betraying Irony' was not, so far as I know, explicitly recognized again until the twentieth century.

This outline of the concept of irony down to the middle of the eighteenth century has been based upon G. G. Sedgewick's *Of Irony, Especially in Drama* (1948) and Norman Knox's *The Word IRONY and Its Context, 1500–1755* (1961), to which the reader is referred.

Later concepts of irony

It was at the very end of the eighteenth and at the beginning of the nineteenth century that the word 'irony' took on a number of new meanings. The old meanings were, of course, not lost, and the old ways of being ironical were not discontinued, though one notices a tendency towards disparaging satiric irony as cheap and vulgar and sceptical irony as cruel, corrosive or diabolic.

The new meanings are new in a number of respects which we can perhaps sort out, but what they add up to is as radical a transformation of the concept of irony as Romanticism was of the worldview of the previous centuries. Where before irony had been thought of as essentially intentional and instrumental, someone realizing a purpose by using language ironically (Example No. 1), it now became possible to think of irony as something that could instead be unintentional, something observable and hence representable in art, something that happened or that one became or could be made aware of (No. 10); from now on irony is double-natured, sometimes instrumental, sometimes observable. Where before irony had been thought of as being practised only locally or occasionally (No. 3), it now became possible to generalize it and see all the world as an ironic stage and all mankind as merely players (No. 11). And where before irony had been thought of as a finite act or at most an adopted manner (as with Socrates), it could now also be thought of as a permanent and self-conscious commitment: the ideal ironist would be always an ironist, alert even to the irony of being always an ironist; irony, in short, could be seen as obligatory, dynamic and dialectical.

The more important of the new meanings that the word 'irony' took on emerged out of the ferment of philosophical and aesthetic speculation that made Germany for many years the intellectual leader of Europe. The principal 'ironologist' of this period was Friedrich Schlegel, but his brother, August Wilhelm, Ludwig Tieck and Karl Solger will also be mentioned.

The first stage, logically if not chronologically, of this new development was to think of irony in terms not of someone being ironical, but of someone being the victim of irony, attention thus shifting from the active to the passive. The victim could be either the butt of an ironic remark, whether made in his absence or not, or the person who has failed to see the irony, whether he is the butt of the irony or not. Once the notion of irony was attached to the naïve or uncomprehending victim of Verbal Irony or some other form of Instrumental Irony, as I shall call it, one could then think of someone as being the ironic, that is, unsuspecting, victim of circumstances or events, these being generally personified. What is new in this is the application of the word 'ironic'; the idea of fortune, for example, as mockingly promising happiness but delivering misery is at least as old as *Le Roman de la rose* (Jean de Meun, *c.*1280) − '*fortune vous moque*'. Friedrich Schlegel, in 1800, speaks of falling unawares into an irony but does so without positing a personified ironic agency. A. W. Schlegel, in 1811, sees Shakespeare as presenting an Irony of Events in his *King Henry V*:

> After his renowned battles, Henry wished to secure his con-
> quests by marriage with a French princess; all that has reference
> to this is intended for irony in the play. The fruit of this union,
> from which the two nations promised to themselves such happi-
> ness in future, was the weak and feeble Henry VI, under whom
> everything was so miserably lost.
>
> (*Lectures on Dramatic Art and Literature* [1809−11],
> trans. John Black, London, 1861, p. 432)

The step that Henry takes to secure his future turns out to be the very step that ensures future disaster. The resemblance of such an Irony of Events to what I have called Instrumental Irony can be made clear by describing, say, ironic praise in similar terms: the word that the butt of the irony takes as flattery turns out on reflec-tion to be the reverse of flattery.

If we think of an Irony of Events in terms of a reversal that takes place in time and of Verbal Irony as a semantic inversion, the way is opened to the application of the word 'irony' to other mentally juxtaposed, that is, observable, inversions, especially those presented to us ready-made in literature. So A. W. Schlegel sees as ironic the way in which Shakespeare undercuts serious scenes by comic, sometimes even parodic, scenes or juxtaposes one charac-ter's favourable self-presentation with another's less flattering estimation of him. He finds a 'secret' irony in Shakespeare's presentation of

> the facility of self-deception, the half self-conscious hypocrisy towards ourselves, with which even noble minds attempt to disguise the almost inevitable influence of selfish motives in human nature.

(op. cit., p. 369)

Ludwig Tieck finds in Shakespeare not only Ironies of Events but also Situational Ironies: 'A very deep irony lies in the scene [in *King Henry IV, Part 2*] in which the prince, at his father's death-bed, puts the crown too hastily on his own head' (Quoted from Ingrid Strohschneider-Kohrs, *Die romantische Ironie in Theorie und Gestaltung*, 1977, p. 133). It is for Tieck a 'deep' irony presumably because Prince Hal, besides mistaking his father's sleep for the sleep of death (a 'superficial' irony) also turns out to be unaware of the motives that led him to make such a mistake. Tieck also finds an irony in Shakespeare's portrait of Brutus: 'he is a most excellent, pure, noble and accomplished man, who wishes nothing but the best; but politically he is blind and weak' (ibid.). The irony lies in Brutus' being blind to his blindness and in his failure to suspect where it will lead him. Later, any accidental or unintentional juxtaposition of opposites was regarded as irony. G. H. Schubert, writing in 1821, saw as irony any naturally occurring incongruity such as, for example, the juxtapositions in the natural scale of rational man and absurd ape, noble horse and ridiculous ass. One of the stock examples of irony in French encyclopaedias is Gautier's 'Quelle ironie sanglante qu'un palais en face d'une cabane!' The (unacknowledged) motive for this semantic extension was undoubtedly the *appearance* of design in these striking juxtapositions.

The next stage was a universalization of these local and particular ironies. It seems to have been only too easy to elevate to metaphysical dignity the ironies of events, large or small, comic or tragic, to which we have all frequently been victims. So we imagine behind these accidents a mocking, capricious, hostile or indifferent deity or destiny. Friedrich Schlegel found it 'strikingly ironic that "*der grosse Maschinist im Hintergrunde des Ganzen*" finally discloses himself as a contemptible Betrayer' (Quoted from G. G. Sedgewick, op. cit., p. 20). In 1833 Connop Thirlwall, in his article 'On the Irony of Sophocles', admits 'that the contrast between man with his hopes, fears, wishes, and undertakings, and a dark, inflexible fate, affords abundant room for the exhibition of tragic irony'. The nineteenth century provided many terms for this generalization of ironies of events: *Ironie des Schicksals, ironie du malheur, du monde, de l'histoire, du sort, de la nature, de nos destinées, de l'existence*, irony of fate, of circumstances, of time and of life. What is new is not the thought that 'We are merely the stars' tennis-balls, struck and bandied / Which way please them', but the use of the word 'irony' in expressing such thoughts.

Similarly, the idea that life is irremediably flawed or even contradictory was not something that first occurred to the Romantics; the use of the word 'irony' in such a context was. A. W. Schlegel, we have seen, speaks of irony in relation to Shakespeare's awareness of 'the *almost inevitable* influence of selfish motives in human nature' (my italics). On the next page he speaks of 'the validity of [Shakespeare's more intelligent spectators'] tacit objections' to idealized representations of human nature, objections Shakespeare has anticipated and acknowledged by allowing 'an occasional glance at the less brilliant reverse of the medal'. The irony for Schlegel lies both in Shakespeare's 'dexterous manoeuvre' and in his 'ironical view' of human relations. He does not, I think, take the further step of seeing as 'objectively' ironic the fact that men are a mix of contradictory qualities.

We have seen the concept of irony enlarged in this Romantic period beyond Instrumental Irony (someone being ironical) to include what I shall call Observable Irony (things seen or presented as ironic). These Observable Ironies – whether ironies of events, of character (self-ignorance, self-betrayal), of situation, or of ideas (for example, the unseen inner contradictions of a philosophical system such as Marxism) – could be seen as local or universal. They were all major developments, not least the development of the concept of *Welt-Ironie*, Cosmic Irony or General Irony, the irony of the universe with man or the individual as victim. But Friedrich Schlegel was to add a further and even more radical development to the concept. With him irony became open, dialectical, paradoxical, or 'Romantic'.

For Schlegel the basic metaphysically ironic situation of man is that he is a finite being striving to comprehend an infinite hence incomprehensible reality. We can call this the Observable Irony of Nature with man as victim. 'The most prominent characteristic of nature', wrote Schlegel, 'is an overflowing and exhaustless vital energy.' He went on to say that nature is infinite both in the 'variety of created forms' and in the 'ever-increasing productiveness of natural life' ('On the limits of the beautiful' in *Aesthetic and Miscellaneous Works*, trans. F. J. Millington, London, 1849, p. 418). Nature is not a being but a becoming, an 'infinitely teeming chaos', a dialectic process of continual creation and de-creation. Man, as but one of these created, soon to be de-created, forms must acknowledge that he can acquire no permanent intellectual or experiential leverage over the whole. He is none the less driven or, as we might now say, 'programmed' to grasp the world, to reduce it to order and coherence, but any expression of his understanding will inevitably be limited, not only because he himself is finite but also because thought and language are inherently systematic and 'fixative', while nature is inherently elusive and protean.

This Observable Irony of man's situation should not be regarded as a hopeless predicament, because it can be countered by an Instrumental Irony. Just as a personified Nature might be said to play with or ironize its created forms, seeming to promise each of them an absoluteness and stability of being only to relativize and destabilize them in the unending flux of creation and de-creation, so man too, or more specifically the artist, being himself a part of nature, has both a creative and a de-creative energy, both an un-reflecting, enthusiastic inventiveness and a self-conscious, ironic restlessness that cannot be satisfied with the finiteness of achievement but must endlessly transcend even what his imagination and inspiration has created. What would really be a hopeless predicament would be a completely comprehensible and therefore, in a sense, dead universe.

The originality and strength of Schlegel's thinking lay in his firm grasp of life as a dialectic process and his insistence that human behaviour is fully human only when it also exhibits an open dynamic dualism. Everywhere in his writing we find him repudiating the Law of Contradiction and denying the value of anything that is not both itself and its self-generated contrary. 'Irony', he says, 'is the form of paradox'; and 'Paradox is the *conditio sine qua non* of irony, its soul, its source, and its principle.' 'Irony is the analysis [as opposed to synthesis] of thesis and antithesis.' 'It is equally fatal for the mind to have a system and to have none. It will simply have to decide to combine the two.'

> [Romantic] irony is the only involuntary and yet completely deliberate dissimulation . . . everything should be playful and serious, guilelessly open and deeply hidden. It originates in the union of *savoir vivre* and scientific spirit, in the conjunction of a perfectly instinctive and a perfectly conscious philosophy. It contains and arouses a feeling of indissoluble antagonism between the absolute and the relative, between the impossibility and the necessity of complete communication.
>
> (Critical Fragment 108 in Peter Firchow, ed.,
> *Friedrich Schlegel's* Lucinde *and the Fragments*, 1971)

Artistic creation, Schlegel argued, has two contrary but complementary phases. In the expansive phase the artist is naïve, enthusiastic, inspired, imaginative; but this thoughtless ardour is blind and so unfree. In the contractive phase he is reflective, conscious, critical, ironic; but irony without ardour is dull or affected. Both phases are therefore necessary if the artist is to be urbanely enthusiastic and imaginatively critical. The artist who can bring off this difficult balancing act, this 'wonderfully perennial alternation of enthusiasm and irony' produces a work that includes within itself its own coming into being. He will be like God or Nature immanent in every finite created element, but the reader will also be aware of his transcendent presence as an ironic attitude towards his own creation. This creative surpassing of creativity is Romantic Irony; it raises art to a higher power since it sees for art a mode of production that is in the highest sense artificial, because fully conscious and arbitrary, and in the highest sense natural, because nature is similarly a dynamic process eternally creating and eternally going beyond its creations. As examples, Schlegel refers frequently to *Don Quixote*, *Tristram Shandy* and Diderot's *Jacques le fataliste*, all works in which the process of composition is integrated into the aesthetic product which in turn is explicitly presented both as art and as (imitation of) life. Paradoxically, this self-parodic self-consciousness makes the work more natural, not less.

Karl Solger's concept of irony rises to even more rarified metaphysical heights than Friedrich Schlegel's, and even those who set out to clarify Solger are not easy to follow. More explicitly than Schlegel, he locates irony at the very centre of life: while the universal, the infinite and the absolute can be manifested only in particular, finite or relative forms, that is, by a self-negation or annihilation, these in turn must 'self-destruct' in the process of fulfilling their function which is to reveal the universal, the infinite and the absolute. The irony resides in the twofold opposed movement in which each sacrifices itself to the other.

The concept of irony as that which restores or that which maintains a balance is found in more familiar terms in A. W. Schlegel, Friedrich's older but intellectually less adventurous brother:

Irony [in drama] . . . is a sort of confession interwoven into the representation itself, and more or less distinctly expressed, of its overcharged one-sidedness in matters of fancy and feeling, and by means of which the equipoise is again restored.

(op. cit., p. 227)

This concept of irony was rediscovered by I. A. Richards, who defines irony, in a similar way, as 'the bringing in of the opposite, the complementary impulses' in order to achieve a 'balanced poise' (*Principles of Literary Criticism*, 2nd edn, London, 1926, p. 250). Closely related is the idea that irony in the form of a balancing self-irony anticipates and guards against a potential (ironic) attack from without. So Friedrich Schlegel speaks of the necessity for ironic self-limitation 'because wherever one does not restrict oneself, one is restricted by the world' (Critical Fragment 37 in Firchow, op. cit.). A. W. Schlegel, as we have seen, noted how Shakespeare by allowing us to glimpse 'the less brilliant reverse of the medal' anticipated an intelligent audience's 'tacit objections' to idealizations. This too turns up again in Richards and also in Robert Penn Warren: 'The poet . . . proves his vision by submitting it to the fires of irony . . . in the hope that the fires will refine it' ('Pure and impure poetry' in R. W. Stallman, ed., *Critiques and Essays in Criticism, 1920–1948*, New York, 1949, p. 103).

The ironist who avoids one-sidedness by dextrously bringing in the opposite position as no less valid may be regarded as having achieved a more or less detached or objective stance. The concept of irony as objectivity is the last (that I shall mention) of the many new meanings or new connotations of the word 'irony' that German Romanticism is to be credited with. Both the Schlegels, as well as Karl Solger and others, used the term in this way. Most dramatists, A. W. Schlegel says, embody their own subjectivity in one character or one viewpoint with which the audience is also supposed to be in sympathy. But Shakespeare, though he endows each of his characters, his 'created forms', with so much life that we cannot doubt that he has entered into their feelings, is at the same time detached from them all and 'soars freely above' the

subjects of his plays, so that they do not express his own subjectivity but collectively 'express the whole world', which, as Goethe
says, is the mark of a real artist.

Yet for A. W. Schlegel, unlike his brother, irony seems always to
have a satiric, moral or reductive function. In speaking of Carlo
Gozzi's fairy-tale dramas he notes the way in which the 'prosaical'
masques ironize the 'poetical' part but does not wonder whether it
could not equally be said that the poetical ironizes the prosaical.
Ironic shrewdness in Shakespeare is admirable but it is 'the grave
of enthusiasm'. In the final count irony leaves the stage when
'tragedy proper' enters, a view one also finds in I. A. Richards.
Solger, however, saw in tragedy an ironizing of the best by something that was still higher, the truth. That at least is how Kierkegaard explains Solger's saying:

> We see heroes beginning to wonder whether they have erred in
> the noblest and finest elements of their feelings and sentiments,
> not only as regards [the] successful issue [of these], but even as
> regards their source and worth. Indeed, what exalts us is the
> destruction of the best itself.

Kierkegaard adds, 'We are not exalted by the destruction of the
great, we are reconciled to its destruction by the fact that truth is
victorious, and we are exalted by its victory' (*The Concept of Irony*,
trans. Lee M. Capel, 1966, p. 334).

The next name in the history of the concept of irony is that of an
Englishman, though an Englishman who had studied German
philosophy and literature. Connop Thirlwall's long article on
irony in Sophocles, referred to above, owes something to German
concepts of irony, but Thirlwall had ideas of his own. He refers to
the long-familiar Verbal Irony and to what he christens Dialectic
Irony, but which is only a new name for the sustained, under-
cutting strategy of a Socratic argument, already recognized as
irony by Cicero. He then introduces the term Practical Irony
which he characterizes as 'independent of all forms of speech' and

of which he says there are 'two totally different kinds'. The first consists in the substitution of ironic actions for ironic words – offering white elephants instead of seeming praise – so that it is still Instrumental Irony. The other covers various types of Observable Irony – the man forced by circumstances to say what he can see being inevitably misunderstood with disastrous effects; the way in which the event reverses our hopes or fears; Clytemnestra rejoicing in her safety when, as the audience knows, her doom is already sealed; the pride of nations that comes before a fall; the ironic contrast of Rome's visible splendours with its inward decay; the dialectic of history, the apparently disastrous fall of one civilization being in fact a desirable consummation, since it makes possible the rise of its more splendid successor; and, finally, differing in kind from all of these, the Double Irony, as Empson was later to call it, of *Antigone* and *Philoctetes*, of court cases and of religious and political factions, in which the immediate opposition is not between a favourable appearance and a grim reality (or vice versa) but between two sides in which both good and bad are mixed.

In recognizing as irony these various situations and events Thirlwall knew that he was using the English word 'irony' in new senses. But these new senses had already been developed in Germany. Hegel, for example, had seen as irony the dialectic progress of history, and before him Solger had liberated irony from its negative associations so that it could be applied to situations and events that seem unpromising but surprisingly turn out fortunate. The Double Irony of *Antigone* is implicit in Friedrich Schlegel's 'tension of opposites' as in, for example, an author's ambivalent attitude towards his characters. And, though it has still earlier origins, Thirlwall's analogy of poet and God reveals the influence of the German theorists:

> The dramatic poet is the creator of a little world, in which he rules with absolute sway, and may shape the destinies of the imaginary beings to whom he gives life and breath according to

any plan that he may choose. . . . From this [mimic] sphere [of his creating] he himself stands aloof.

(Connop Thirlwall, 'On the Irony of Sophocles',
Philological Museum, Vol. II, 1833, pp. 490–1)

What is new in Thirlwall is a specifically English concept of Dramatic Irony, the irony of a character's utterance having unawares a double reference: to the situation as it appears to him and, no less aptly, to the situation as it really is, the very different situation already revealed to the audience. Ironic in this sense is Aegisthus' utterance in *Electra*:

> Surely, O God, there is example here
> Of righteous retribution.

He thinks the body before him is that of his enemy. It is in fact that of his wife. What is valuable in Thirlwall is less his originality than his clear exposition and his generous offering of examples; these made his essay a major landmark in the history of the concept of irony in English, establishing the terms 'irony of fate' and Sophoclean (or Dramatic) Irony. The term Practical Irony was ill-chosen and had no success.

The reader who, with the prospect of a century and a half of theorizing about irony still before him, is already saying, as Friedrich Schlegel had already said, 'What gods will rescue us from all these ironies?' will be relieved to hear that Thirlwall's article was the last major step in the long history of the concept of irony. All the principal kinds of irony that have been practised and all the classes of phenomena that we now regard as ironic have been, more or less clearly, recognized as irony. Nearly everything since can be classed either as restatements, rediscoveries, distinctions between 'real' and 'so-called' irony, clarifications, classifications or sub-classifications; or can be regarded as more general discussions of the nature of irony, its place in man's intellectual and spiritual life and its place in relation to other literary modes. Kierkegaard's thinking on irony from his 1841 thesis, *The*

Concept of Irony, onwards, is directed very largely towards a placing of irony between what he calls the aesthetic and the ethical 'stages' of spiritual development. For Kierkegaard 'whoever has essential irony has it all day long'; he is not ironical from time to time or in this or that direction but considers the totality of existence *sub specie ironiae* and is never ironical in order to be admired as an ironist. For Amiel, irony is Philosophical or General; he has a concept of a law of irony: 'Absurdity is interwoven with life: real beings are animated contradictions, absurdities brought into action' (*Journal Intime*, 15 November 1876). For Heine, Baudelaire, Nietzsche and Thomas Mann irony is principally Romantic Irony, but Heine is also aware of the self-protective function of irony, an awareness that looks back to Theophrastus' portrait of the eiron and forward to some twentieth-century objections to irony. Where Hegel's 'universal irony of the world' was dialectic, and negative only within a larger progression − 'God lets men do as they please with their particular passions and interests; but the result is the accomplishment of − not their plans but his' (quoted from G. R. G. Mure, *A Study of Hegel's Logic*, Oxford, 1950, p. 257) − Heine's was nihilistic, 'the great Author of the universe' was an Aristophanes crushing mankind under his 'giant wit'. But Heine saw a (non-progressive) dialectic in *Don Quixote*: Sancho Panza and his master, allegories of body and soul, ironize each other through their mutual incompatibility. Samuel Butler and his friend Miss Savage delighted in what they called unconscious humour or unconscious irony, terms for the involuntary revelation of one's real attitudes or beliefs: as when a hospital medico speaks, as one did recently, of 'some 800 patients [per year being] subjected to intensive care'. In 1902 Jules de Gaultier used the term *bovarysme* for the way people can think of themselves as other than they are, specifically the way they cast themselves as the heroes and heroines of romances. *Bovarysme* is clearly a kind of irony and might have been recognized as such had the French at that time developed the concept of irony as far as the Germans and the English.

If in the post-Romantic nineteenth century the dominant concept was that of nihilistic irony, the dominant twentieth-century concept seems to be that of an irony that is relativistic and even non-committal. We read that irony is 'a view of life which recognized that experience is open to multiple interpretations, of which no *one* is simply right, and that the co-existence of incongruities is part of the structure of existence'. (Samuel Hynes, *The Pattern of Hardy's Poetry*, Chapel Hill, N.C., 1961, pp. 41–2). Although this definition allows us to see Shakespeare's irony as A. W. Schlegel saw it, that is, as a detached, clearsighted objectivity, free from *parti pris*, it also opens the way to relativism and eventually to a concept of irony that hardly distinguishes it from ambiguity or even a fear that one might be thought to have said something. Roland Barthes, in *S/Z*, says that Flaubert,

> in wielding an irony fraught with uncertainty, brings about a salutary uneasiness in the writing: he refuses to halt the play of codes (or does so badly), with the result that (and this is no doubt the true test of writing as writing) one never knows whether he is responsible for what he writes (whether there is an individual subject behind his language): for the essence of writing (the meaning of the work which constitutes writing) is to prevent any reply to the question: who is speaking?
>
> (Quoted in Jonathan Culler, *Structuralist Poetics*, London, 1975, pp. 158–9)

Irony in this latest sense is a way of writing designed to leave open the question of what the literal meaning might signify: there is a perpetual deferment of significance. The old definition of irony – saying one thing and giving to understand the contrary – is superseded; irony is saying something in a way that activates not one but an endless series of subversive interpretations. We shall clearly have to return to this curious notion. At the popular level, the level of newspaper reporting, for example, 'irony' is likely to be used of coincidences or when there is a very small margin between success and failure in a matter of great moment:

> An early rescue party had passed only metres from the spot where the three youths had collapsed on Sunday night. A further irony was that the State Emergency Service helicopter scanned the site early on Monday, but had been unable to see through the dense scrub and bush.
>
> (*The Age*)

In writing this section I have found especially useful Norman Knox's article on irony in Philip P. Wiener, ed., *Dictionary of the History of Ideas*, Vol. II, 1973, and the opening chapter on Romantic Irony in Anne K. Mellor's *English Romantic Irony*, 1980.

3
The anatomy of irony

Basic features

Looking back at the almost cancerous growth of the concept of irony since the 1790s, we might well ask what, if anything, still holds it together. Is there a single common feature or perhaps a set of family resemblances some of which show up in all instances of irony and only in irony? If we cannot show that there is, we cannot have a coherent concept of irony or identify the features that distinguish one kind of irony from another. This chapter will constitute a search for both common and differentiating features, drawing upon the examples of irony at the end of chapter 1 but not exclusively upon these.

APPEARANCE AND REALITY

'The basic feature of every Irony is a contrast between a reality and an appearance' (Haakon Chevalier, *The Ironic Temper*, New York, 1932, p. 42). Is this borne out by our examples? Michael Frayn, Chaucer, Butler, Gay, Orwell, the kings of Siam and Sarah N. Cleghorn (Nos 1–6) all more or less plausibly pretend to be saying or doing one thing while really conveying a quite different message. Hastings, Dr Johnson and the Roman plebs (Nos 7 and 10) have all confidently but very mistakenly assumed that things are as they seem to be or will turn out as expected. The composer of the death notice and Carson McCullers' Portia (Nos 8 and 9) both thought that the sentiments they expressed were perfectly proper; we can see in both expressions unsuspected meanings of contrary import. Hardy (No. 11) explicitly points to the irony of mistaking for Non-verbal Irony on God's part what is really impersonal cosmic indifference. (If 'some mean, monstrous ironist / *Had* built this mistimed fabric of the Spheres / To watch the throbbings of its captive lives', the ironic contrast would then have been between what God seemed, to orthodox believers, to be doing and what he really was doing.) In No. 12a there is an appearance of design; we feel that such a blatant incongruity could not happen by chance, and yet it has. In No. 12b our naïve assumption, which the irony corrects, might be that it is guilt that is to be punished not innocence. In No. 13 Thirlwall himself points out what seems to be and what really is the case. In No. 14 our mistaken assumption is that the world is sensibly arranged; but now we're told that the more an actor practises his craft, the worse he must become and that time, in teaching us how to live wisely, takes away the power to live at all. The comic strip joke (No. 15b) appears to make sense: at the level of what the strip represents – a region purporting to be part of the real world – a way in does imply a way out, and things do happen by mistake. But created characters cannot sensibly leave or refer to the fiction of which they are constitutive elements. Moreover, the artist, in pretending to disparage his own art gives us grounds for admiring it.

'Reality', as the word is used here, is to be taken as meaning only what the ironist or the ironic observer sees as such. Someone who has heard of Dr Johnson but does not know whether *Tristram Shandy* has lasted or not could only guess at an irony. Those Christians who can 'rest back' and contemplate the everlasting frying of human souls will miss Carson McCullers' real point. In Anatole France's allegorical history, the irony of the words 'The Penguins had the finest army in the world. So had the Porpoises' consists in the revelation, by means of contradiction, that what appear to be statements of fact are really, in Anatole France's opinion, empty boasts or subjectively determined beliefs.

Not everything that is other than it seems to be is an instance of irony:

He thought he saw an Argument
That proved he was the Pope:
He looked again, and found it was
A Bar of Mottled Soap.
                    (Lewis Carroll, *Sylvie and Bruno Concluded*,
                                        London, 1893, p. 319)

Nor is every way of saying one thing in order to mean another: Spenser wrote 'Duessa' but meant 'Roman Catholicism'. The relationship between appearance and reality is, in other words, neither an unlikeness nor a likeness or equivalence but, as Chevalier says, a contrast (or an opposition, contradiction, contrariety, incongruity or incompatibility).

EIRON AND ALAZON; PRETENCE AND CONFIDENT UNAWARENESS

Deceptions, such as lies, hoaxes, hypocrisy, white lies and equivocations, which purport to convey a truth but do not, may also be seen as contrasts of appearance and reality. But since they are not thought of as irony, it is evident that irony has some other element or elements besides this contrast. That irony and deception are close neighbours is clear from the Latin for irony: *dissimulatio* (as well as *ironia*). In Theophrastus both the Eiron and Alazon were dissemblers, the one concealing himself behind evasive, noncommittal, self-depreciative masks, the other behind a façade of boasts. But the modern ironist, whether he plays an eironic or an alazonic part, dissembles or rather, pretends, not in order to be believed but, as has been said, in order to be understood. In deceptions there is an appearance that is proffered and a reality that is withheld, but in irony the real meaning is meant to be inferred either from what the ironist says or from the context in which he says it; it is 'withheld' only in the weak sense that it is not explicit or not meant to be immediately apprehensible. If among an ironist's audience there are those who are not meant to understand, then what we have in relation to them is a hoax or an equivocation, not an irony, though their non-apprehension may well enhance the pleasure of the irony for the real audience. Insinuations and innuendoes, where the person addressed is invited to complete by inference what has been left unsaid, may be intended to inform or to mislead – 'He was at Cambridge with Burgess and all that lot' – or may be irony, as in

> Alice is marrying one of the guard.
> 'A soldier's life is terrible hard.'
> > Says Alice.
> > (*When We Were Very Young*)

where A. A. Milne's real meaning is in the inferable relationship of cause and effect between the two statements, an inference beyond the reach of the child narrator who nevertheless juxtaposes them.

In what I have called Observable Irony – for example, the irony of the robber robbed – there is no ironist and hence no ironic pretence. It seems, however, that the name of irony got attached to situations of the robber robbed kind by the intermediary of a belief in a supernatural agency or a personified and hostile Fate, Life or Fortune. Othello saw the ignorant cuckold as the victim of diabolic irony:

> O, 'tis the spite of hell, the fiend's arch-mock,
> To lip a wanton in a secure couch,
> And to suppose her chaste.
> > (IV, i, 70–2)

And we are still inclined to say, when we are in a great hurry to go out and a shoelace breaks, 'That's just the sort of thing that would happen', as if there were things that maliciously will themselves to happen. But since we can and do see situations and events as ironic without any reference to a non-human ironist behaving like the kings of Siam, it follows that ironist and ironic pretence are basic features only of Instrumental Irony.

On the other hand, it is only in Observable Irony, it seems, that we have alazony and the alazon, alazony being defined as the confident unawareness found in or imputed to the alazon, the victim of irony. (The Alazon in Theophrastus is only a boaster. But it is notorious that such people tend to deceive themselves more than those to whom they boast and come to believe their own inventions.) Portia's alazony consists in her self-assured blindness to the double standard of her Christianity. The alazony of the Roman plebs consists in their simple belief that you can get rid of an enemy by exiling him. So the Americans drove Fidel Castro into the arms of the Russians. The alazony of Antigone and Creon consists in their obstinate blindness to the validity of, respectively, civil and kinship obligations. In some cases the alazon and the alazony have no more actual existence than a shadow or after-image. First we see that something is ironic, for example a palace found facing a hovel, and this dazzling irony creates the after-image of the alazony or totally defective sense of irony that would permit or fail to reflect upon such a state of affairs. Alternatively, one may think of such ironies as if they were Instrumental, that is, *as if* someone had tendentiously brought about a striking incongruity. Here it is the ironist who is hypothetical, not the alazon. In either case to say that such a simple incongruity, however striking, is irony is probably to use the word in a weakened sense.

Alazony varies widely in several respects. The alazon may be totally unreflective, or boldly confident; or he may be infinitely circumspect, seeing every trap but the one he falls into. We may see him as highly blameworthy, like Charles the wrestler in *As You Like It* – 'Where is this young gallant that is so desirous to lie with his mother earth?' – or as forgivable, like Catherine in *Northanger Abbey*; we may even quite illogically and 'unfairly' impute alazony: Milne's fictional Alice is a victim of irony because her remark 'A soldier's life is terrible hard' is made *as if* she were serenely unaware of the presence of the previous line – 'Alice is marrying one of the guard' – and so equally unaware of the effect produced by the juxtaposition. But of course the juxtaposition exists only in the poem not in the fictional world in which she has made her innocent remark. We can even see an alazony in a blue wren's attempt to drive off the aggressive blue wren he sees reflected in a bedroom window. An alazon's confidence may be fully explicit as when, confidently anticipating and prophesying the end of the world, one gives away all one's property, or it may be fully implicit: 'Rather funny, I mean to say', Bertie Wooster says, when a policeman, the alazon in this case, has his helmet stolen, 'a chap who's supposed to stop chaps pinching things from chaps having a chap come along and pinch something from him.'

The position is different with Instrumental Irony. Here, instead of an alazon really unaware that his language or behaviour in a certain context is incongruously at odds with the situation as the observer sees it, we have an ironist pretending unawareness. While making sure (in ways yet to be discussed) that his real meaning will be inferable, he will write as if he has never doubted what he seems to be saying nor ever suspected that what he is really saying could be inferred. This air of sincerity, this plausible manner, coupled with the unacceptability of *what* is apparently being put forward, resembles the naïvety of the real alazon or victim of Observable Irony. Confirmation of this resemblance is found in the not infrequent confusion or uncertainty that arises: Evelyn Waugh has spoken of the 'sly, complacent smile' of the *Mona Lisa*; but 'sly' is appropriate only to an ironical Mona Lisa, while 'complacent' would be appropriate only to a naïve Mona Lisa ironized by Leonardo. The reviewer of a new translation of *The Tale of Genji* writes, 'It is one of the charms, and difficulties, of the book that the reader is never quite sure whether Murasaki is being suavely ironic or merely naïve.' W. V. O'Connor classes Sarah N. Cleghorn's poem (No. 6) as 'Naïveté', 'a special form of irony half way between verbal and dramatic irony' ('Irony' in Alex Preminger *et al.*, eds, *Princeton Encyclopedia of Poetry and Poetics*, London, 1974). The poem ironically praises the convenient siting of the golf links and/or simply presents the ironic situation of a world of reversed values. The Vietnam War slogan 'Kill a Commie for

Christ today' can be taken as a brilliant ironic parody of a certain extreme right brand of American Fundamentalism or as a real slogan seriously intended and so constituting for an ironic observer a Self-betraying Irony of the kind Carson McCullers presents (No. 9). Whether the ironist plays the mock-modest or mock-circumspect role of the eiron or the mock-confident role of the alazon, he is to some extent playing a role; in writing as he does he implies a naïve writer who resembles the alazon of Observable Irony.

DRAMATIC STRUCTURE

Until an ironic message is interpreted as intended it has only the sound of one hand clapping. In other words, Instrumental Irony is a game for two players (though that is not all it is). The ironist, in his role of naïf, proffers a text but in such a way or in such a context as will stimulate the reader to reject its expressed literal meaning in favour of an unexpressed 'transliteral' meaning of contrasting import. This may sometimes be fully expressible; 'What a nice clean face!', for example, offers no serious challenge. But generally (see Nos 2, 3, 5, 6) the transliteral meaning is better thought of as a 'latent semantic sphere' as Lene Petersen calls it (in her 'Le strutture dell'ironia ne La Coscienza di Zeno di Italo Svevo', *Revue Romane*, special number 20, 1979, p. 15; see also Wayne C. Booth – 'The act of reconstruction . . . cannot really be *said*, it must be *performed*.' – *A Rhetoric of Irony*, Chicago, 1974, p. 39). The game is played out when there is, to use Aristotle's terms, not only a peripeteia or reversal in the reader's understanding but also an 'anagnorisis' or recognition of the ironist and his real intent behind the pretence. The interpretation of non-ironic insinuations and innuendoes differs from this in that there is recognition but no reversal.

The following diagrams show, in a simplified form, the processes of conveying and interpreting Instrumental Irony.

Roles and messages

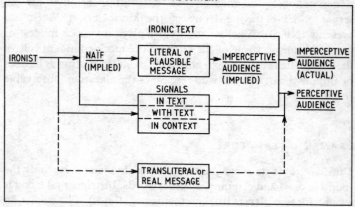

Notes

1 The roles in the 'drama' of irony are underlined. But there is one role not shown, that of the butt or object of the irony: who or what the ironist is ironizing. Roles may be combined: naïf and object, very often; ironist and object, as in self-irony; object and audience (perceptive or imperceptive), e.g. *Gulliver's Travels* where Gulliver = (English)man = reader; ironist and audience, as when an ironist speaks ironically for his own private pleasure; object and imperceptive audience, e.g. Mr Collins as Mr Bennet's butt in *Pride and Prejudice*. An actual imperceptive audience is not found in all irony.

2 Signals may be part of the text (e.g. contradictions and exaggerations) or may accompany the text (e.g. gestures). Alternatively or additionally the ironist may be able to rely upon his audience having the same values, customs or knowledge as himself; the general unacceptability of cannibalism allows Swift to signal his ironic intent in *A Modest Proposal* only briefly and fleetingly. It may be misleading to label as 'signals in context' this reliance on a common socio-cultural referential system. Christine Kerbrat-Orecchioni ('Problèmes de l'ironie', *Linguistique et Sémiologie*, Travaux du Centre de recherches linguistiques et sémiologiques de Lyon, 1976, Vol. II, p. 30) says, however, that 'the interpretation of irony brings into play, besides their linguistic competence, the cultural and ideological competences of ironist and audience' and Wayne C. Booth (op. cit.,

pp. 43–4) says, 'In reading any irony worth bothering about, we read life itself. . . . We read character and value, we refer to our deepest convictions.'

3 The ironist conveys his real message to his audience only in the sense that he provides them with the means for arriving at it. Hence the dotted lines.

'Coding' and 'decoding'

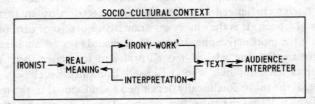

SOCIO-CULTURAL CONTEXT

Notes

1 By 'irony-work' (cf. Freud's '*Witzarbeit*' or 'joke-work') is meant (a) the transformation of the real meaning or intent into the ironic message, e.g. blame transformed to seeming praise; (b) the establishment of the required degree of plausibility; (c) the provision of signals (if any).

2 'Text' here comprises the plausible message together with any 'in-text' and 'with-text' signals, all of which the audience as interpreter will read in the common socio-cultural context.

3 Interpretation 'reverses' the irony-work: motivated by the signals or the clash of message and context, the interpreter dismisses the plausibility and transforms praise to blame, thus arriving at the ironist's intent.

There is an equivalent dramatic structure in Observable Irony, but generally in a weak form, the roles of the ironist and the audience-interpreter being fused into one: the observer with a sense of irony. We can still say there is both anagnorisis and peripeteia in seeing something as ironic since what is involved is a re-interpretation of something (an event, a situation, a state of affairs, an attitude, a belief or an idea); the ironic observer recognizes or discovers that this something can be seen as really the reverse, in some sense, of what it has appeared to be at first glance or to eyes less sharp or minds less informed. In Ironies of

Events, where the reversal is in time, the dramatic structure need by no means be weak: in *King John* the French prince and the papal legate each expresses his confidence in the other's support or obedience; and each finds his expectations reversed.

Most Observable Ironies come to us ready-made, already observed by someone else and presented fully-formed in drama, fiction, film, paintings and drawings, proverbs and sayings, so that the role of the audience or reader is much less active than that of the reader challenged to a game of interpretation by an Instrumental Ironist. It is the observant dramatist, novelist or cartoonist who is the more active one. Irony, Kierkegaard says, 'is not present in nature for one who is too natural and too naïve, but only exhibits itself for one who is himself ironically developed. . . . Indeed, the more polemically developed an individual is, the more irony he will find in nature' (op. cit., pp. 271–2). To see something ironic in life is to present it to oneself as ironic. (If one is an artist one then presents it to others.) This is an activity that demands, besides a wide experience of life and a degree of worldly wisdom, a skill, allied to wit, that involves seeing resemblances in things unlike, distinguishing between things that seem the same, eliminating irrelevancies, seeing the wood in spite of the trees, and being alert to connotations and verbal echoes. It follows that, strictly speaking, the irony is only potentially in the phenomenon and is actualized only when the ironic observer represents it to himself or the ironic author presents it to others. The term 'Observable Irony', therefore, lacks philosophical rigour, as most terms do.

There is a street in Paris named Impasse de l'Enfant Jésus. To see this as ironical one need only be (unlike him who named it) sensitive to the incompatible connotations of 'impasse' and 'Jesus'; but the irony is enhanced if one recalls the Gospel of St John: 'Jesus saith unto him, I am the way . . . no man cometh unto the Father, but by me' (14:6). A sense of irony involves not only the ability to see ironic contrasts but also the power to shape them in one's mind. It includes the ability when confronted with anything at all, to imagine or recall or notice something which would form an ironic contrast. Matthew Arnold, faced with the 'exuberant self-satisfaction' of Sir Charles Adderley and Mr Roebuck saying:

> 'Such a race of people as we stand, so superior to all the world! The old Anglo-Saxon race, the best breed in the whole world! I pray that our unrivalled happiness may last! I ask you whether, the world over or in past history, there is anything like it?'

confronts it with a paragraph he came across by chance in a newspaper:

> A shocking child murder has just been committed at Nottingham. A girl named Wragg left the workhouse there on Saturday morning with her young illegitimate child. The child was soon afterwards found dead on Mapperly Hills, having been strangled. Wragg is in custody.
>
> ('The function of criticism at the present time',
> *Essays in Criticism*, London, 1884, pp. 22–3)

The effect, as was intended, is that of an ironic contrast. Chance provided Arnold only with the possibility of bringing into ironic juxtaposition a complacent and a disturbing picture of nineteenth-century England; it was Arnold's sense of irony which brought them together, so constituting an ironic situation. Similarly, Arnold's incidental comment on the ugliness of the name 'Wragg' – 'In Ionia and Attica they were luckier in this respect . . . by the Ilissus there was no Wragg, poor thing!' – can be given an ironic connotation at Arnold's expense by recalling that infanticide was not unknown in Attica and that Plato even recommended it (in certain circumstances) for his ideal republic.

We can draw two conclusions from these examples. One is that there is nothing that a 'polemically developed' ironist with a well-stored mind could not see as ironic if he wished; there is always somewhere a contrasting context. Thus the role of the ironic observer is more active and creative than the word 'observer' suggests. The other is that while we may legitimately question whether or not something has been said or done with ironical intent, we cannot question anyone's right to see something as ironic. We may question his sense or taste though.

AFFECT

We have isolated as basic to all irony a contrast of 'appearance' and 'reality'. Something that is only apparent implies either error or pretence and from this we derived the alazony of Observable Irony and the pretended naïvety of Instrumental Irony. The Aristotelian concepts of recognition and reversal were employed to characterize the dynamic quality of irony as a movement from an appearance to a contrasting 'reality'. This led incidentally to an identification of the roles involved in irony either as a game for two or as a mode of apprehension for the 'ironically developed'.

What has yet to be considered is whether or not there is some special feeling-quality that is attached to irony and that ought to form part of its definition. It will be readily agreed that particular ironies may affect us very strongly but also very differently: the painful irony of *Othello*, the apparent insult that turns out to be a witty compliment, the comical misunderstandings of a Feydeau farce, or the two mental asylum patients in Beckett's *Watt* who agreed, 'after an exchange of views', that it was in 'seizing suddenly a plump young rat', whose confidence they had gained by feeding it frogs and baby thrushes, and giving it to other equally tame rats to eat that they 'came nearest to God'. As literary critics, moreover, we shall generally find more to interest us in the qualities peculiar to each instance than in any quality or qualities common to all. As literary theorists, we might agree with Norman Knox ('On the classification of ironies', *Modern Philology*, August 1972, pp. 53–62) that there are several classes of irony – tragic, comic, satiric, absurd or nihilistic, paradoxical – each of which has its own 'philosophical-emotional colouring'.

None the less, I think it may be argued that there is at least one feeling-quality common to all instances of irony and that this is not something that is obliterated by the emotional colouring peculiar to classes or to instances of irony. Irony, I would say, is a topic for discussion only because it is one thing and not several things, and it is something we value because, as audience-interpreters or observers, it gives us a special pleasure and not because it brings us pleasures of different kinds. In other words, I do not think we should ever have felt the need to apply the word 'irony' to such a range of phenomena if this had depended upon a merely intellectual recognition of the basic features set out in the first paragraph of this section.

Allan Rodway ('Terms for Comedy', *Renaissance and Modern Studies*, Vol. VI, 1962, p. 113) says that 'irony is not merely a matter of seeing a "true" meaning beneath a "false", but of seeing a double exposure . . . on one plate.' But though we see the 'false' as false, it is, and it must be if there is to be irony, presented as true. Interpreting Swift's *A Modest Proposal* is not a process that entails discarding the literal meaning; it is still there in all its plausibility. Oedipus was mistaken in thinking he had escaped his fate; but his sense of the situation as he saw it was real. An accomplished Instrumental Ironist will aim at achieving maximum plausibility for his ostensible meaning; an accomplished author presenting Observable Ironies will aim at lending his alazonic characters maximum conviction: Lady Macbeth will not say 'A little water clears us of this deed' as if she had grave doubts. It is not only in Double or Paradoxical Irony – as in Corneille's *Le Cid* where we feel as equally obligatory and absolute the opposed demands of Love and Honour – but in all irony that we are confronted with co-existing but irreconcilable, irrelatable 'realities'. However often we return to *Macbeth* or to an Instrumental Irony we have 'seen through', we enjoy once again that curious special feeling of paradox, of the ambivalent and the ambiguous, of the impossible made actual, of a double contradictory reality.

It is the absence of this feeling that distinguishes irony from what is too heavy or too light to deserve the name. A sarcasm such as 'You are a nice sort of friend!' is not for a moment plausible in its literal sense; the tone conveys reproach so strongly that no feeling of contradiction is possible. At the other extreme come the texts that fail to provide the reader with grounds for a correct interpretation, either through incompetence or through perverseness or malice, as when Flaubert spoke of his writing his *Dictionnaire des idées reçues* in such a way that the reader could not tell for sure whether he was being made a fool of or not (letter to Louis Bouilhet, 4 September 1850). Here, in relation to the bourgeois reader he has in mind, Flaubert is a hoaxer or equivocator not an ironist, but for readers like Bouilhet the irony is clearly characterized by the necessary sense of contradiction.

It may be conceded, to Knox, that this feeling of paradox is of special importance to what he calls Paradoxical Irony but not that it is unimportant elsewhere. Perhaps we can at this point suggest that there is a second feeling, a feeling of liberation, characteristic of, though not peculiar to, irony and that the two feelings vary inversely with one another, the second being more important in the other classes of irony Knox lists: tragic, comic, satiric and nihilistic. We can group these together as Closed Ironies, so called because each points to the 'reality' that definitively unmasks the appearance, though without affecting the latter's plausibility or verisimilitude. (Paradoxical Irony is Open in the sense that the 'reality' that closes it is a view of the world as inherently contradictory or open! Creon and Antigone, the Penguins and the Porpoises confront each other to eternity.)

I am not at all sure that 'liberation' is the right or the only word for this second feeling. Perhaps what we need is a constellation of psychologically related terms any one of which may be the best suited in a particular case. One of these would be comedy. Freud regarded (Instrumental) irony as 'very close to joking . . . and . . . among the sub-species of the comic. . . . It produces comic pleasure in the hearer, probably because it stirs him into a contradictory expenditure of energy, which is at once recognized as being unnecessary' (*Jokes and their Relation to the Unconscious*, trans. James Strachey, revised Angela Richards, Harmondsworth, 1976, p. 232).

In this it resembles jokes, which 'liberate pleasure by getting rid of inhibitions' (p. 185). G. G. Sedgewick (*Of Irony, Especially in Drama*, 1948, p. 5) says of irony that 'its force derives from one of the keenest and oldest and least transient pleasures of the reflective human mind – the pleasure in contrasting Appearance with Reality.' That it is, as in Freud, a comic pleasure is clear from the fact that he doesn't exclude 'grim humour' from tragic situations in which there is irony. Of course *Othello* and *Oedipus Rex* are not comedies. They are, however, spectacles of blindness, and calling them tragedies cannot take from them what they have in common with blind-man's buff: comic pleasure with overtones of sadism and voyeurism. As for those who say that the tragic (that is, the pitiful and the terrible) and the comic are mutually exclusive either in life or in literature, they are themselves blindly moving about in worlds not realized and might well be asked

> Where were you when I laid the [heart's] foundations?
> Tell me, if you know and understand.
> Who settled its dimensions? Surely you should know.
>
> (Job 38:4–5)

Where was Fontenelle when he ridiculed as 'digne de la comédie' the scene in Racine's *Britannicus* in which Nero, from a concealed position, forces Junie to praise him and behave coldly to her lover Britannicus in order to save the latter's life?

The word 'comic' suggests a certain 'distance', psychologically speaking, between the amused observer and the comic object; the word 'liberation' suggests 'disengagement', 'detachment', and these in turn 'objectivity' and 'dispassion'. Taken together they constitute what might be called the archetypal Closed Irony stance characterized emotionally by feelings of superiority, freedom and amusement and symbolically as a looking down from a position of superior power or knowledge. Goethe says that irony raises a man 'above happiness or unhappiness, good or evil, death or life'. Amiel compares 'the feeling which makes men earnest [with] the irony which leaves them free', and Thomas Mann speaks of irony as

> an all-embracing crystal-clear and serene glance, which is the very glance of art itself, that is to say: a glance of the utmost freedom and calm and of an objectivity untroubled by any moralism.
>
> ('The Art of the Novel' in *The Creative Vision*, ed. Haskell M. Block and Herman Salinger, 1960, p. 88)

In Lucretius, Lucan, Lucian, Cicero, Dante, Chaucer, Shakespeare, Bacon, Heine, Nietzsche, Flaubert, Amiel, Tennyson, Meredith, not to mention the Bible, we can find the idea that looking down from on high upon the doings of men induces laughter or at least a smile.

The ironic observer's awareness of himself as observer tends to enhance his feeling of freedom and induce a mood of satisfaction, serenity, joyfulness, or even exultation. His awareness of the victim's unawareness leads him to see the victim as bound or trapped where he feels free; committed where he feels disengaged; swayed by emotions, harassed, or miserable, where he is dispassionate, serene, or even moved to laughter; trustful, credulous, or naïve, where he is critical, sceptical, or content to suspend judgement. Where his own attitude is that of a man whose world appears real and meaningful, he will see the victim's world as illusory or absurd. Distinguishing the different kinds of heroes in fiction, Northrop Frye writes, 'If inferior in power or intelligence to ourselves, so that we have the sense of looking down on a scene of bondage, frustration, or absurdity, the hero belongs to the *ironic* mode' (*Anatomy of Criticism*, 1957, p. 34). From this point of view the pure or archetypal ironist is God – 'He that sitteth in the heavens shall laugh: the Lord shall have them in derision' (Psalms 2:4). He is the ironist *par excellence* because he is omniscient, omnipotent, transcendent, absolute, infinite and free. The archetypal victim of irony is, *per contra*, man, seen as trapped and submerged in time and matter, blind, contingent, limited and unfree – and confidently unaware that this is his predicament.

Dozens of examples might be cited in which the gods are imagined as the spectators in a theatre or a cockpit, as puppet-masters, or as playing a game in which men are toys, cards or pawns. These could all be matched with images of the artist as this sort of god analogously related to his 'creation'. Friedrich Schlegel writing of Goethe's *Wilhelm Meister* says: 'The author himself seems to take the characters so lightly and whimsically, scarcely ever mentioning his hero without irony and smiling down upon his masterpiece itself from the height of his spirit' ('Über Goethes Meister', 1798, in *Kritische Ausgabe*, Vol. II, Hans Eichner, Paderborn and Munich, 1967, p. 133). James Joyce echoes Flaubert in emphasizing the ironic distance that the author as *dieu caché* should maintain from his creation.

These feelings of superiority, detachment, amusement and satisfaction that characterize irony, especially what I have called Closed Irony, may reflect the temperament of some ironists and devotees of irony. One ought, however, to distinguish between the feelings that motivate the ironist and are recreated in his readers and the feeling-quality of the irony itself. Swift felt the lacerating effect of savage indignation but his irony plays it cool in even his bitterest work, his 'modest proposal' that the English Protestant landlords in Ireland should restore the country to economic health by buying and eating the babies of the destitute unemployed Catholics:

> As to our City of *Dublin*, Shambles may be appointed for this purpose, in the most convenient parts of it, and Butchers we may be assured will not be wanting, although I rather recommend buying the Children alive, and dressing them hot from the Knife, as we do *roasting Pigs*.
>
> (Jonathan Swift, *A Modest Proposal*)

A feeling that might most naturally have found expression in a howl of anguish and despair has here been transformed into a rationally argued economic treatise coloured only by the modest proposer's complacent, self-congratulatory tone. Swift has been able to control the impulse to blurt out what he feels: there has been a pause, a distancing, an intellectualizing, and, in the end, while nothing could have had a greater emotional impact, something has been made as well as said.

Anatole France once coupled irony and pity. The irony he valued, he said, was an irony qualified by gentleness and benevolence. Others have sought a closer relation, a concept of irony in which sympathy was an essential ingredient and no less so than detachment. Thomas Mann, for example, in his Goethe novel *Lotte in Weimar* and elsewhere, sees irony as both diabolic and divine, nihilistic and all-embracing, objective and loving. Doubtless he knew of a similar development in Friedrich Schlegel where, as we have seen, the enthusiastic creativity that was complementary to an ironic self-delimiting could also be seen as one aspect of a wider, dialectic understanding of irony. It is probably inevitable in a self-critical, relativist age, that irony should thus develop from a 'closed' state to this 'open' or ambivalent, paradoxical state, in which it is both detached and involved, critical and sympathetic. We have even come to see that there may be dangers in irony as defined by Thomas Mann:

> that irony which glances at both sides, which plays slyly and irresponsibly – yet not without benevolence – among opposites, and is in no great haste to take sides and come to decisions [which] may prove premature.
>
> ('Goethe and Tolstoy' in *Essays of Three Decades*, trans. H. T. Lowe-Porter, London, 1947, p. 173.)

Open or Paradoxical Irony tends, as Kierkegaard and Wayne Booth have shown, to develop galloping relativism, from which it can be saved, at least in theory, by a call to order in the form of renewed ironic laughter from on high, but more probably by the practical exigencies of life.

Variable features

In the process of tracing the evolution of the concept of irony and establishing the basic features, some distinctions between classes of irony have already emerged, notably those between Instrumental and Observable Irony and between Closed and Open (or Paradoxical) Irony. The term Paradoxical Irony was proposed by Knox ('Irony', *Dictionary of the History of Ideas*, Vol. II, 1973, p. 627) who lists four other classes and distinguishes all five from each other on the basis of three criteria (which, however, I modify somewhat):

1 Attitude towards the victim of the irony, ranging from a high degree of detachment to a high degree of sympathy or identification.
2 Fate of the victim: triumph or defeat.
3 Concept of reality: whether the ironic observer thinks of reality as reflecting his values or as hostile to all human values.

These give us the four Closed Ironies:

I Reality reflects observer's values:
  (a) '*Comic irony* ['comic' in the happy-ending sense] reveals the triumph of a sympathetic victim.' (That his confidently gloomy expectations are defeated makes his situation comic in the ordinary sense as well.)
  (b) '*Satiric irony* reveals the defeat of an unsympathetic victim.'
II Reality hostile to all human values (defeat therefore inevitable):
  (c) '*Tragic irony*, sympathy for the victim predominates.'
  (d) '*Nihilistic irony*, satiric detachment counterbalances or dominates sympathy, but a degree of identification always remains since [the observer] necessarily shares the victim's plight.'

The fifth class of Paradoxical Irony is open or ambivalent in respect of sympathy (there might, for example, be two opposed victims equally sympathetic), outcome (a defeat that is also a triumph), and concept of reality ('everything is relative: reality in part does and in part does not reflect human values'). Knox does not distinguish between Instrumental and Observable Irony, but it is clear that he is thinking in terms of the latter. Equivalents to (a) and (b) in terms of Instrumental Irony would be, for example, 'blaming in order to praise' and 'praising in order to blame'. There could be no 'Instrumental' equivalents to (c) and (d) because a reality defined as hostile would fail to authenticate the ironist's real meaning.

In the rest of this section the variable features I shall be concerned with are those that affect the quality of irony. We can ask what makes one situation or event more ironic than another and also what can be done to heighten the irony of a dramatic situation or improve the rhetorical or artistic effect of an ironic style. I take it for granted that one cannot be interested in irony and indifferent to the quality of irony; my attempt in the last section to argue that the basic features of irony include certain feeling-qualities has already implied this. In so far as I shall be talking of ways of enhancing irony, I may seem to be prescribing rules to artists, a questionable enterprise, artists being defined as those who know how to break with advantage the rules of art. So anything in what follows that may look like such a rule is to be understood as prefaced by the words 'other things being equal'.

A rhetorically effective, an aesthetically pleasing, or simply a striking irony owes its success, it would seem, largely to one or more of a small number of principles and factors. Some of these seem to be aspects of a more general principle that I cannot identify.

THE PRINCIPLE OF ECONOMY

Stylistically speaking, irony is dandyism, whose first aim, as Max Beerbohm, ironist and dandy, tells us, is 'the production of the supreme effect through means the least extravagant'. The accomplished ironist will use as few signals as he can. He will not denounce the evils of historical inveracity when, with Jane Austen, he need only say that he thinks 'Truth . . . very excusable in an Historian'. Like a ju-jitsu wrestler or a catalyst he will act only to set in action the self-destructive potential of his opponent: parody, the *reductio ad absurdum*, ironic agreement, advice and encouragement, the rhetorical question and several other ironical tactics can all be seen as this kind of economy of effort. The ironist who hides his attack behind a mask of naïvety or insensibility is saying that intelligence and sensitivity are not needed to demolish so feeble an adversary.

In Observable Irony the same principle is at work. The engineer is hoist with his *own* petard. The wax that glued Icarus' feathers and enabled him to fly from Crete is, as it melts in the sun, re-employed as the cause of his fall: 'Thrift, thrift, Horatio!' The principle of economy seems operative even when the engineer is hoist with another's petard provided that both the victim and the victimizer can in some way be seen as one and the same. So it is ironic when the wicked become themselves the victims of wickedness and more ironic when a criminal practising a highly specific crime becomes a victim of another in precisely the same game. It is as if he had, economically, fallen into his own trap.

THE PRINCIPLE OF HIGH CONTRAST

Another way of explaining why it is ironic for a robber to be robbed or a swimming instructor drowned is to point to the unlikelihood of this, that is, to the disparity between what might be expected and what actually happens. The wider the disparity, the greater the irony: 'Into what pit thou seest / From what height fallen.' Ironic contrasts take many forms: trivial cause and momentous outcome (For want of a nail . . . the battle was lost); great expectations and anti-climax (*Parturient montes, nascetur ridiculus mus*); enormous effort to achieve the highest goal foiled at the very last minute and by the merest chance. Or the disparity may be between the inevitability of an outcome or certainty of a fact and an *appearance* of indeterminacy, randomness or open possibilities. What Knox calls Nihilistic Irony may be enhanced by increasing the injustice, the disparity between guilt and undeserved reward, or innocence and punishment.

This principle of high contrast applies also to the alazon. Instead of widening the gap between appearance and reality or expectation and event, one can magnify the alazon's blind confidence or the circumspection, ingenuity or perseverance he shows in trying to avoid the unavoidable. Assurance and circumspection may be contraries, but in an alazon they amount to the same since his circumspection has a blind spot precisely where it should not. The irony may be enhanced by showing the alazon not only confident or diffident but explicitly so. Costard in *Love's Labour's Lost* assures Berowne at length that three threes are not nine.

THE POSITION OF THE AUDIENCE

In the theatre particularly, the quality of the irony depends very much on whether the audience already knows the outcome or true state of affairs or learns of these only when the victim learns. In the former case the irony is a spectacle of blindness and can be further enhanced if the victim's utterances are applicable not only to the situation as he sees it but also to the situation as the reader or audience knows it to be. So in Arnold's poem, Rustum confronts his son Sohrab (each concealing his own and ignorant of the other's identity) and says:

> For well I know that did great Rustum stand
> Before thy face this day, and were reveal'd,
> There would be then no talk of fighting more.
>
> (*Sohrab and Rustum*, 370–2)

On the stage this device of discrepant awareness, to borrow a term from Bertrand Evans' *Shakespeare's Comedies* (Oxford, 1960), can be varied in several ways: the audience alone may grasp the full import of what is said; one or more of the characters may know in full or in part what the audience knows; a character who is in the dark may either speak or hear in ignorance what is to his advantage or disadvantage; the presence of a character may be concealed from one or more or all of the other characters; such a concealed character may be in the know or in the dark; and he may address the audience or simply see or overhear what may be to his advantage or disadvantage. In the most tensely ironic scenes that I can recall from either comedy or tragedy the audience sees A, who is concealed, B, who knows of the concealment but must not betray any knowledge of it though anxious to prevent C, ignorant of the concealment, from saying what will antagonize A and bring harm to himself and B. Such a scene may be found in *The School for Scandal* and *Britannicus*. Notwithstanding all that, there are effective ironies in which the audience is kept in the dark. Shirley Hazzard, in her *Transit of Venus* (New York, 1980), plays a neat trick on the reader by letting him know that a character who has just said to the heroine 'Us ordinary folks can tell more or less how things are likely to go on with us' is going to die three months later in a plane crash but not letting him know until the end of the novel that the heroine will be on the same plane.

TOPIC

Other things being equal, ironies will be more or less forceful in proportion to the amount of emotional capital the reader or observer has invested in the victim or the topic of the irony. Saying that does not mean leaving the realms of art and irony and entering those of pure subjectivity and individual preference; the areas of concern that most readily generate irony are, for the same reason, the areas in which most emotional capital is invested: religion, love, morality, politics and history. The reason is of course that such areas are characterized by inherently contradictory elements: faith and fact, flesh and spirit, emotion and reason, self and other, ought and is, theory and practice, freedom and necessity. To exploit these ironically is to enter an area in which the reader is already involved.

4
The practice of irony

Verbal Irony

In this final chapter I shall look, selectively, at irony in action, and in this section at Instrumental Ironies in which language is the instrument. As we shall see, it is not always possible to distinguish Instrumental Irony from the presentation of Observable Irony, but in general the distinction is clear: in Instrumental Irony the ironist says something in order to have it rejected as false, *mal à propos*, one-sided, etc.; in presenting an Observable Irony the ironist presents something ironic – a situation, a sequence of events, a character, a belief, etc. – that exists or is to be thought of as existing independently of the presentation.

A rhetorician dogged enough could probably identify as many ways of being ironical as there are ways of using words. I shall confine myself to the commoner varieties of Verbal Irony, in a great many of which the basic technique is either that of 'going along with' the ironic butt and placing him in high relief or that of depreciating oneself, which is the countersinking or intaglio method.

The simplest form of 'high-relief' verbal irony is the antiphrastic praise for blame, for example the 'Congratulations!' we offer to the 'smart Alec' who has let the side down. This can be elaborated in a number of directions. Probably the best known instance of ironic agreement in English literature is in Chaucer's presentation of the worldly monk:

> And I seyde his opinion was good.
> What sholde he studie and make hymselven wood,

> Upon a book in cloystre alwey to poure,
> Or swynken with his handes, and laboure,
> As Austyn bit? How shal the world be served?
>   (*The Canterbury Tales, General Prologue*, 183–7)

Swift's *Directions to Servants*, his satire of the faults and follies of servants, takes the form of advising them to do what they too frequently already do and reproducing their lame excuses as valid reasons: 'In Winter Time light the Dining-Room Fire but two Minutes before Dinner is served up, that your Master may see, how saving you are of his Coals.' In his *L'Esprit des lois*, Montesquieu ineptly defends slavery:

> The peoples of Europe, having exterminated those of America, had to enslave those of Africa so as to have someone to clear all that land.
> Sugar would be too dear if one didn't have slaves to cultivate the sugar-cane.
> The peoples in question are black from head to foot; and their noses are squashed so flat that it is next to impossible to feel any pity for them.
> One cannot bring oneself to think that God, who is so wise and judicious, would put a soul, and above all a virtuous soul, into a body that is black all over.

>   (Book XV, Chapter 5)

Hyperbole is the most obvious device for 'setting up' what is being attacked. One of the most glorious examples in English must be in Chaucer's *The Merchant's Tale*. January, the 'worthy knyght' of this tale, takes it into his head, at the age of sixty, to be married; his praise of wives and marriage runs to no fewer than 130 lines:

> To tak a wyf it is a glorious thyng,
> And namely whan a man is oold and hoor;
> Thanne is a wyf the fruyt of his tresor.
> Thanne sholde he tak a yong wyf and a feir,   (1268–71)

For who can be so buxom as a wyf?
Who is so trewe, and eek so ententyf
To kepe hym, syk and hool, as is his make?
For wele or wo she wole hym nat forsake;   (1287–90)

A wyf! a, Seinte Marie, *benedicite*!
How myghte a man han any adversitee
That hath a wyf? Certes, I kan nat seye.   (1337–9)

She kepeth his good, and wasteth never a deel;
Al that hire housbonde lust, hire liketh weel;
She seith nat ones 'nay,' whan he seith 'ye.'
'Do this,' seith he; 'Al redy, sire,' seith she.   (1343–6)

As the 'worthy knyght' is presented as sincere in what he says, what we have, strictly speaking, is an Observable Irony. Since, however, it is presented by the unhappily married Merchant, we can easily imagine him retailing January's long blazon with a bitter irony (which Chaucer perhaps intends us to find amusing).

The *reductio ad absurdum* ends, by definition, with the destruction of the opponent's position; but it begins as if the position were tenable at least. A good brief example is Brecht's poem, 'The Solution', on the workers' rising in 1953, which 'brings out' very effectively the latent contradiction in East Germany's claim to being a people's democracy:

After the rising of the 17th June
The Secretary of the Writers' Association
Had leaflets distributed in the Stalinallee
In which you could read that the People
Had lost the Government's confidence
And could only win it back
By redoubled efforts. If so, would it not
Be simpler, if the Government
Dissolved the People
And elected another?

('The Solution' trans. Martin Esslin, *Encounter*, June 1959, p. 60)

In 1756 Soame Jenyns' *Free Inquiry into the Nature and Origin of Evil* offered to explain human misery with the hypothesis of 'superior beings . . . who have power to deceive, torment, or destroy us, for the ends only of their own pleasure or utility', thus treating us as we treat lower animals (*The Works of Soame Jenyns*, London, 1790, Vol. III, p. 72). Such unprofitable speculation provoked Dr Johnson into a continuation:

> I cannot resist the temptation of contemplating this analogy, which, I think, he might have carried further, very much to the advantage of his argument. He might have shown, that these 'hunters, whose game is man', have many sports analogous to our own. As we drown whelps and kittens, they amuse them-selves, now and then, with sinking a ship, and stand round the fields of Blenheim, or the walls of Prague, as we encircle a cockpit. As we shoot a bird flying, they take a man in the midst of his business or pleasure, and knock him down with an apoplexy. Some of them, perhaps, are virtuosi, and delight in the operations of an asthma, as a human philosopher in the effects of the air-pump. To swell a man with a tympany is as good sport as to blow a frog. Many a merry bout have these frolick beings at the vicissitudes of an ague, and good sport it is to see a man tumble with an epilepsy, and revive and tumble again, and all this he knows not why. As they are wiser and more powerful than we, they have more exquisite diversions; for we have no way of procuring any sport so brisk and so lasting, as the paroxysms of the gout and stone, which, undoubtedly, must make high mirth, especially if the play be a little diversified with the blunders and puzzles of the blind and deaf.

Then, taking a wider view, Johnson brings Jenyns himself on to the stage:

> One sport the merry malice of these beings has found means of enjoying, to which we have nothing equal or similar. They now and then catch a mortal, proud of his parts [and] fill [his head]

with idle notions, till, in time, they make their plaything an author [of] a treatise of philosophy. Then begins the poor animal to entangle himself in sophisms, and flounder in absurdity, to talk confidently of the scale of being, and to give solutions which himself confesses impossible to be understood.

(*Dr Johnson's Works*, London, 1825, Vol. VI, pp. 64–6)

The opportunity should not be missed of pointing out that here Johnson has not only written ironically but has also created an ironic situation of a highly instructive kind: the 'merry malice' of his ironic treatment of Jenyns' blind confidence in his 'idle notions' sets up a threefold analogy of life, theatre and irony; the ironist is a 'superior being', superior beings look on life as a comedy, as a 'play . . . diversified with the blunders and puzzles of the blind and deaf', and to mount such a comedy is to practise irony. What Johnson has given us is a marvellous model or archetype of what I have called Closed Irony with its affinities with the exercise of knowledge and power and its overtones of (non-sexual) voyeurism and sadism. One is reminded of Nietzsche's saying that 'existence could be justified only in aesthetic terms': 'According to the primitive logic of feeling (but is our own so very different?) any evil was justified whose spectacle proved edifying to the gods' (Friedrich Nietzsche, *The Birth of Tragedy* and *The Genealogy of Morals*, trans. Francis Golffing, New York, 1956, pp. 9 and 201).

One is also going along with the ironic butt, though in a weaker sense, if instead of exalting his merits one minimizes his defects. The commonest form of this ironic strategy is understatement; here Kierkegaard presents the obviously absurd not as the pinnacle of philosophical insight but merely as not quite satisfactory:

Dear Reader: I wonder if you may not sometimes have felt inclined to doubt a little the correctness of the familiar [Hegelian] philosophic maxim that the external is the internal, and the internal the external.

(*Either/Or*, trans. David and Lillian Swenson, New York, 1959, p. 3)

Michael Frayn's allusions to such 'small slips' as the Government's forced repatriation to the USSR and Stalin's mercy of a million Russian fugitives are also of interest here. In *Gulliver's Travels* Swift presents the (obviously unjustifiable) causes of war in the tone appropriate to matters of no importance:

> Sometimes the Quarrel between two Princes is to decide which of them shall dispossess a Third of his Dominions, where neither of them pretend to any Right. Sometimes one Prince quarreleth with another, for fear the other should quarrel with him.
>
> (Book IV, Chapter 5)

The rhetoricians have a term 'preterition', which can be applied to the ironic pretence either not to mention something ('Far be it from me to say anything here of your . . .') or that it is not worth mentioning: when the chateau has burnt down with all its paintings and furnishings, stables and granges, the agent in the Paul Misraki song reports

> mais à part ça, Madame la Marquise,
> Tout va très bien, tout va très bien.

The intaglio method isolates the butt or object of the irony not by promoting him or it but by demoting oneself, playing the eironic not the alazonic naïf. A simple example of this tactic which goes back to Socrates is in Charles Rycroft's *A Critical Dictionary of Psychoanalysis* (Harmondsworth, 1972, p. ix): 'Since the author [i.e. Rycroft himself] suffers from the not uncommon constitutional defect of being incapable of understanding Jung's writings . . .' Under the same general heading come pretended doubt where nothing is doubtful, pretended error or ignorance, and pretended apologies, deference or astonishment:

> Now is nat that of God a ful fair grace
> That swich a lewed mannes wit shal pace
> The wisdom of an heep of lerned men?
> (*The Canterbury Tales*, General Prologue, 573–5)

In the following passage Gibbon satirizes the exploits of biblical heroes by pretending to accuse those with 'objections against the authority of Moses and the prophets' of scepticism, ignorance, narrow-mindedness, petulance, heresy and puritanism:

> There are some objections against the authority of Moses and the prophets which too readily present themselves to the sceptical mind; though they can only be derived from our ignorance of remote antiquity, and from our incapacity to form an adequate judgement of the Divine economy. These objections were eagerly embraced and as petulantly urged by the vain science of the Gnostics. As those heretics were, for the most part, averse to the pleasures of sense, they morosely arraigned the polygamy of the patriarchs, the gallantries of David, and the seraglio of Solomon. The conquest of the land of Canaan, and the extirpation of the unsuspecting natives, they were at a loss how to reconcile with the common notions of humanity and justice. But when they recollected the sanguinary list of murders, of executions, and of massacres, which stain almost every page of the Jewish annals, they acknowledged that the barbarians of Palestine had exercised as much compassion towards their idolatrous enemies as they had ever shown to their friends or countrymen.
>
> (*The Decline and Fall of the Roman Empire*, Chapter 15)

There are other recognized ways of being ironical which do not obviously involve pretending either to accept the victim's position or to be incapable of grasping it. When Dryden wanted, by way of revenge, to call Sir Robert Howard's play *The Duke of Lerma* undramatic and unoriginal, he did it like this:

> To begin with me – he gives me the compellation of *The Author of a Dramatique Essay*, which is a little discourse in dialogue, for the most part borrowed from the observations of others: therefore, that I may not be wanting to him in civility, I return him his compliment by calling him *The Author of the Duke of Lerma*.
>
> (*Defence of an Essay of Dramatic Poesy*)

This is ironic innuendo; the reader must first see the implied resemblance between the play and the essay before he can see that the compliment is an ironical one. In the following passage John Bayley ironizes F. R. Leavis by describing Iago in language that is unmistakably the language in which Leavis might be described. Having quoted Leavis' harsh criticism of Othello, Bayley continues:

> We might notice at this point the odd irony that those who decline to be taken in by Othello find themselves in the company of Iago. Iago too is in no doubt about Othello's real nature, and he is not a tolerant man: his opinions about life, morals, and society are very definite indeed. Moreover his tone suggests now and then that though he has 'placed' Othello he remains exasperated with him, indeed envious of him, for although Othello's masterfulness and nobility are a fraudulent pretence they are imposed with such maddening conviction and success upon the world at large.
>
> (*The Characters of Love*, London, 1960, p. 129)

This too could be called innuendo or, to distinguish it from the previous example, irony by analogy: what seems to be an exposure of A is really or also an exposure of B whose resemblance to A has to be inferred. *The Beggar's Opera*, *Animal Farm* and other satirical allegories are also irony by analogy.

It is commonly said that a writer is being ironical when in fact what he is doing is presenting (or creating) something that he has seen as ironic; in other words we also see as Verbal Irony the verbal presentation of Observable Irony. This usage can be defended on the ground that such a presentation usually involves similar verbal skills. As explained in the section (in chapter 3) on the dramatic structure of irony, what I have called Observable Ironies exist only potentially in the phenomena observed and become actual only through presentation; the more skilful the presentation the clearer the ironical situation 'observed'. A good example can be found in Günter Grass' *The Flounder*:

What ideological contradictions provide whom with dialectical (in the Marxengelsian sense) entertainment when in a Communist country ['the People's Republic of Poland'] the state power gives orders to fire on workers, thirty thousand of them, who have just been singing the Internationale outside the party building in proletarian protest?

(Trans. Ralph Manheim, Harmondsworth, 1979, p. 114)

It is clear that this was written in a way that brings out the contradictions. It would have seemed barely ironic at all if it had read: 'As the protesting shipyard workers (who were singing the Internationale) gave no signs of dispersing, the authorities were obliged to give orders to fire. It is estimated that there were at the time about thirty thousand workers in — Street where the party building is located.' On the other hand, Grass could have enhanced the contradictions by adding that the orders to fire on the workers were given to and obeyed by other workers, the people's army and the people's police.

There is another way of being ironical which can equally well be regarded as the creating of an Observable Irony. This is when the eironic naïf, a mere shadow in the Gibbonian 'One is at a loss to understand', is given a seemingly independent dramatic existence as an *ingénu* who may ask questions or make comments the full import of which he does not realize. The effectiveness of this ironical mode comes from its economy of means; mere common sense or even simple innocence or ignorance may suffice to see through the complexities of hypocrisy or expose the irrationality of prejudice. The following example comes from a rather third-rate sketch of Mark Twain's, *Little Bessie Would Assist Providence*:

'Mama, why is there so much pain and sorrow and suffering? What is it all for?'
'It is for our good, my child. In His wisdom and mercy the Lord sends us these afflictions to discipline us and make us better. . . . None of them comes by accident.'
'Isn't it strange? . . . Did He give Billy Norris the typhus?'
'Yes.'

'What for?'

'Why, to discipline him and make him good.'

'But he died, mama, and so it couldn't make him good.'

'Well, then, I suppose it was for some other reason. . . . I think it was to discipline his parents.'

'Well, then, it wasn't fair, mama . . . *he* was the one that was punished. . . . Did He make the roof fall in on the stranger that was trying to save the crippled old woman from the fire, mama?'

(Quoted from Norman Foerster, ed., *American Poetry and Prose*, 4th edn, Boston, 1957, pp. 1048–9)

The *ingénu* in eighteenth-century literature is very frequently a non-European, a visitor from China or Persia or a Red Indian, Tahitian or Brobdingnagian, who does not, like us, see the world through the obscured or distorting spectacles of creeds, customs and conventions but freshly with the eyes of common sense or rationality. For example, the Tahitian Orou in Diderot's *Supplement to Bougainville's Voyage* is hard put to it to understand the Roman Catholic concept of priestly celibacy.

For a twentieth-century *ingénu* we can go to J. D. Salinger's *The Catcher in the Rye*. The hero, Holden Caulfield, is presented as an inarticulate, sub-literate, 'sad screwed-up' adolescent, totally incapable of getting his life together. Nevertheless we are meant to see that he has a good eye for what is phoney in other people and that his own values are sound even when he thinks they are not:

'You know what the trouble with me is? I can never get really sexy – I mean *really* sexy – with a girl I don't like a lot. I mean I have to *like* her a lot. If I don't, I sort of lose my goddam desire for her and all. Boy, it really screws up my sex life something awful. My sex life stinks.'

(Harmondsworth, 1958, p. 153)

This confession leads to his being advised to visit a psychoanalyst, advice which we translate as Salinger's way of implicating psycho-analysis in the degradation of sexual morality in contemporary America.

There is a straight line of development here from simple Verbal Irony − 'How stupid I must be not to see what everyone else takes for granted!' − to the complex fictional character presented as seemingly stupid or immature. But the roles of irony in fiction will be discussed later.

Irony in the theatre

In this and the next section I shall try to show that the theatre and narrative fiction both tend to generate irony. There will be much overlap in the kinds of irony generated, but broadly speaking the kinds of irony most typical of plays are not the kinds most typical of novels.

In what follows the words 'theatre' and 'theatrical' will often be used of the visual or rather the spectacular element in drama, the immediate stunning impact, the 'show' of showbiz. This suggests straight away a link with irony because it is the audience that sees and the dramatis personae who are seen, who are unaware of being observed, blind to the fact of being watched. Characters are not infrequently literally blind or blinded and almost invariably are metaphorically blind, whether wilfully or accidentally, to the machinations of the villain, the wiles of the hero or heroine, the workings of fate, the identity of another, or their own natures or motives. All this the audience sees. Blindness and sightedness − ironically reversed in Tiresias and Oedipus (the blind 'seeing' and the sighted 'blind') and in Gloucester ('I stumbled when I saw') − are as basic to theatre as to irony.

In contradistinction to 'theatre' and 'theatrical', the words 'drama' and 'dramatic' will sometimes be used in the popular sense of 'exciting' or 'gripping'. The stage is a place where something is about to happen or be revealed. Since the audience feels this but the dramatis personae generally do not, there is a basic potential for irony inherent in drama. Moreover, what is about to happen is something that is going to happen to the unsuspecting dramatis personae. Their blindness therefore has reference to the future as well as to the present. What also needs to be stressed here is that the dramatis personae, though they are only fictions, are impersonated by actual flesh and blood. To these physical presences the audience cannot help responding with varying intensities of sympathy and antipathy that are complicated by the awareness of the separation of their worlds. So there is both a physical intimacy and a psychological distance, and consequently there is the possibility of reinforcing the impact of the play with certain questionable pleasures well known to psychology: the pleasure of playing God or secretly manipulating other people's lives; the pleasures of exhibitionism, both in dressing up and stripping off; the pleasures of voyeurism, of watching people exposing themselves; and the pleasures of sadism – the theatre has always been a theatre of cruelty, an arena. Some of these pleasures we have already associated with irony and all of them require both a degree of sympathetic identification and a degree of psychological dissociation.

'Theatre' and 'drama' are also distinguished from each other in another way. 'Theatre' is the wider term, taking in both the physically enabling conditions for drama (stage, off-stage, auditorium, etc.) and the activities immediately involved in putting on a play (rehearsing, producing, performing and seeing it). Drama is the narrower term, the focus of these activities, the play that is being performed. The distinction is necessary because I want to suggest that the ironies we find in plays get there through a tendency in drama to 'theatricalize' itself. By that I mean that much of the form and thematic content of drama can be seen as internalizations and transformations of the immediate theatrical context of plays; the dramatist and his script, the actors with their costumes and make-up, the stage itself, the director and the *mise en scène* (including rehearsals and performance), and the auditorium and audience, all tend to find themselves inside plays in more or less disguised forms. As long ago as 1953 Susanne Langer suggested that in film the media was the message and she correlated the moving camera which, free of time and space, becomes the mind's eye with the elements of the dreamlike in the films themselves (*Feeling and Form*, London, pp. 411–15). The disembodied nature of the screen image and the isolating darkness of the cinema auditorium are also 'dreamlike'. For Hollywood and other 'dream factories' it was 'natural' that the thematic content of films should be an internalization of the conditions of their production and reception.

Theatre, drama and irony are interrelated in many ways. Even a brief ironical remark, in being both a challenge and a response, is drama in miniature with both peripeteia and anagnorisis, both reversal in the addressee's understanding and recognition of the ironist's real intent. Moreover, in being ironical, the ironist can be seen as putting on a one-man show: he assumes his role of naïf and speaks, writes or behaves as if he really were the sort of person who might hold the views the irony is intent on destroying or subverting. The ironist will aim at the highest degree of plausibility for what he seems to be saying; similarly, the actor presenting, say, Brutus will aim at making a Brutus who is credible in his own terms. The ironist will also aim at the highest degree of clarity for the simultaneous retraction or exposure of his pretended meaning, for example by suggesting a context of contrary import or employing a fallacious argument; similarly, the playwright will aim at showing us the 'real' Brutus, that is, not Brutus as self-defined and as presented by the actor but Brutus as the whole play defines him and as the audience comes to see him as they reconcile the various contradictions and anomalies that arise either within the character or in his relationships to others or the world at large.

So the difference between Instrumental Irony and drama in which there is ironic characterization could be seen as simply a difference of technique. The ironist makes a sort of actor of himself in assuming his role of naïf while the dramatist employs actors in the role of 'real' alazons, victims of Observable Ironies in being, as Brutus was, not the sort of persons they think they are. Not every play, of course, ironizes its characters or ironizes them equally; *Twelfth Night* treats Malvolio worse than *The Cocktail*

Party treats Sir Henry Harcourt-Reilly, regrettable though that may be.

Much closer than Instrumental Irony to being dramatic or theatrical is Observable Irony. Ironies of Event, for example, which operate in time, have a clear dramatic structure, the typical case involving a victim with certain fears, hopes or expectations who, acting on the basis of these, takes steps to avoid a foreseen evil or profit from a foreseen good; but his actions serve only to lock him into a causal chain that leads inevitably to his downfall. This abstract description of the Irony or Events would also serve for the bare bones of the plot of a tragedy, such as *The Bacchae*, *King Lear* or *The Revenger's Tragedy*. The earliest recognition of the dramatic force inherent in the peripeteia of an Irony of Events is in the *Poetics* though of course Aristotle does not use the word 'irony':

> Indeed, even chance occurrences seem most remarkable when they have the appearance of being brought about by design – when, for example, the statue of Mitys at Argos killed the man who had caused Mitys's death by falling down upon him at a public entertainment.

> (1452a)

This anecdote is perhaps best known in its dramatized form in *Don Giovanni*.

All Observable Ironies are by definition 'theatrical' in that the presence of an 'observer' is necessary to complete the irony. Irony is not just something that happens; it is something that is at least picturable as happening. We may say it is ironical for someone to be cheated by the person he intended to cheat, but in order to be able to say this we must already have constructed a mental theatre with ourselves as the unobserved observer clearly seeing the situation as it really is and also to some degree feeling the force of the victim's confident unawareness.

This contrast between the single and limited vision of the victim of irony and the double, complete vision of the ironic observer is also found in the real theatre. First, we can think of the dramatis personae as being like the victim of irony. As the Father in Pirandello's *Six Characters in Search of an Author* says (speaking for the characters and addressing the producer), 'We, as ourselves, have no other reality outside this illusion! . . . What other reality should we have? What for you is an illusion that you have to create, for us . . . is our sole reality' (trans. Frederick May, London, 1954, p. 55). The audience, for its part, is like the ironic observer. It enters imaginatively into the dramatic illusion but it also stands outside the play and judges it as a performance: evaluating *this* production, recognizing the actors, pleased or displeased with the casting, or the sets, or the cuts in the text. From this point of view there is only a potential irony in drama, but it can be actualized by giving a character lines which, unknown to him, have an additional reference outside his little world. For example, we would not say that it is ironical that Shakespeare's Cassius never for a moment suspects that he is a character in *Julius Caesar* though the audience knows that he is. The potential irony here is actualized only when he says:

> How many ages hence
> Shall this our lofty scene be acted over,
> In state unborn, and accents yet unknown!
>
> (III, i, 111–13)

This sort of thing, quite common in Shakespeare, has an extremely odd effect, a *Verfremdungseffekt*, since it makes us more sharply aware of Cassius' unawareness of his simultaneous existence as a Roman and as an actor speaking in accents now known of 'accents yet unknown'!

There is a second and stronger sense in which we can say that drama, though not necessarily ironic, is typically so. Just as the ironic observer of a situational irony sees the victim behaving in confident unawareness of the real state of affairs, so, in most plays, the audience will know more of what is going on than the dramatis personae. In many plays the audience will already know what the outcome will be from the prologue or the programme notes or the title or previous performances or from earlier versions in literature or legend or from history. Consequently it will see the dramatis personae possessed by mistaken or unnecessary hopes, fears, convictions, etc. Even in plays about which the audience has no advance knowledge, it will generally soon know more than the dramatis personae since the audience is always present, but the dramatis personae see and hear at most only what takes places when they are on the stage.

I have suggested that irony is essentially both theatrical and dramatic though in some respects only in a weak sense. I have suggested, too, that drama is at least typically ironic and perhaps essentially ironigenic, that is, productive of irony; Kenneth Burke more or less 'equates' drama, dialectic, irony and peripeteia (*A Grammar of Motives*, Cleveland and New York, 1962, pp. 503–17), and it is not easy to think of a play from Aeschylus to Arrabal in which there is no ironic structure or no ironic situations or events. But now I want to move into a more speculative area with the hypothesis that the nature of drama is such that plays tend to be ironical as a result of internalizing one or more elements of their immediate theatrical environment or context, that is, the necessary pre-conditions and material supports of the plays themselves as listed at the beginning of this section.

Internalization is not something found only in plays. There is the song that conventionally internalizes the singer:

> Early one morning, just as the sun was rising,
> I heard a maid sing in the valley below:
> 'Oh, don't deceive me! Oh, never leave me!
> How could you use a poor maiden so?'

There are the no less conventional invocations that no longer have, if indeed they ever had, their extra-literary and preconditional status as prayers. The envoy is an internalized postscript or dedication. There are novels that internalize in various ways the business of writing a novel; in *Tristram Shandy*, the author, the mode of composition, the readers and the critics are all included.

But I think it is fair to say that such internalizations are less varied than those in drama because novels, songs and poems have so much less context to internalize. Cinema and television, in this respect, are closer to drama.

In drama the most widely recognized, because least transformed, internalizations are those of production and performance, namely the rehearsal play and the play-within-the-play. But one can also identify internalizations of the playwright, the director, the actor, the audience and the script. Each of these internalizations is associated with a distinct type of irony.

THE REHEARSAL PLAY AND THE PLAY-WITHIN-THE-PLAY

In England the heyday of the rehearsal play and the play-within-the-play seems to have been the Restoration-Augustan period with an average of one a year, of one or other of them, from 1671 to 1738 – though of course they are found both earlier and later and in other countries. Plays, masques or other theatrical productions are mounted in eight of Shakespeare's plays, and there are three or four informal performances in other plays of his, as well as a host of concerted deceptions such as the exposure of Parolles in *All's Well that Ends Well*. The internalizing theatre of one dramatist alone, Pirandello, has been the subject of a great number of studies, and half a dozen monographs on the play-within-the-play in French, English, Spanish and German theatre attest to the importance of this genre.

Each of the hundreds of rehearsal plays and play-containing plays will have its own specific qualities and purposes, and I would not want to seem willing to ignore these. But my concern here is with the special ironic effects that result from turning a play outside in, bringing into the dramatic illusion those things, the production and performance whose function it is to create the illusion. The effect of this internalization is to set up a dialectic between our imaginative response to the play as mimesis or illusion and our critical or aesthetic response to the play as play or artefact.

By writing a play containing a second, and explicit, illusion, Pirandello or Shakespeare or Sheridan or Stoppard reinforces the illusion at the primary level but simultaneously makes us see it as an illusion: when, in the passage from *Six Characters* quoted above, the Father addresses the Producer as a producer, one of Pirandello's effects would be quite lost if we didn't see that this Producer is himself being produced by a real producer and is as much a character as the Father. With the suicide at the end of the play, Pirandello has us wondering whether the Boy is 'dead' only at the level of the play being rehearsed or 'really dead' at the level of the rehearsal being played, the whole situation being complicated by the play's insistence that art is more real than life.

The irony involved in these plays that draw attention, explicitly or implicitly, to their status as play, to their illusory nature, is Romantic Irony. In Romantic Irony the inherent limitation of art, the inability of a work of art, as something created, fully to capture and represent the complex and dynamic creativity of life is itself imaginatively raised to consciousness by being given thematic recognition. The work thereby transcends naïve mimesis and acquires an open dimension that may invite us to further speculation. Having dismissed the masque his magic has created, Prospero, who has been stage-managing most of the action of *The Tempest*, likens the whole world to the masque, and by implication, Shakespeare's implication, we see *The Tempest* and Prospero himself in the same light:

> These our actors,
> As I foretold you, were all spirits, and
> Are melted into air, into thin air;
> And, like the baseless fabric of this vision,
> The cloud-capp'd towers, the gorgeous palaces,
> The solemn temples, the great globe itself,
> Yea, all which it inherit, shall dissolve,
> And, like this insubstantial pageant faded,
> Leave not a rack behind. We are such stuff

> As dreams are made on; and our little life
> Is rounded with a sleep.
>
> (IV, i, 148–58)

But not every play-containing play exemplifies Romantic Irony. It
is clear enough that the theme of *A Midsummer Night's Dream* is
the imagination's power over perception, the play itself being its
own prime instance, but in *Hamlet* it is not so clear in spite of
Hamlet's reflections upon the power of dramatic illusion.

At a lower level, plays of these kinds may employ irony to
satirize dramatic conventions. In the following passage from
Sheridan's *The Critic, or A Tragedy Rehearsed*, the satiric point is
made by having Puff, the author of the tragedy, naïvely fail to
distinguish between the play and the presentation of the play:

> SIR WALTER. Philip, you know, is proud Iberia's king!
> SIR CHRISTOPHER. He is.
> SIR WALTER. His subjects in base bigotry
> And Catholic oppression held, – while we,
> You know, the Protestant persuasion hold.
> SIR CHRISTOPHER. We do.
> SIR WALTER. You know, beside, his boasted armament,
> The famed Armada, by the Pope baptized,
> With purpose to invade these realms—
> SIR CHRISTOPHER.   Is sailed,
> Our last advices so report. . . .   (II, ii, 80–96)
>
> SIR WALTER.   You also know—

> *Dangle.* Mr Puff, as he *knows* all this, why does Sir Walter go
> on telling him?
> *Puff.* But the audience are not supposed to know anything of
> the matter, are they?
> *Sneer.* True, but I think you manage ill: for there certainly
> appears no reason why Sir Walter should be so communicative.
> *Puff.* 'Fore Gad, now, that is one of the most ungrateful

observations I ever heard – for the less inducement he has to tell all this the more, I think, you ought to be obliged to him.

(II, ii, 110–20)

THE PLAYWRIGHT, THE DIRECTOR

Internalizations of playwrights and directors without their plays are less obvious because in such cases they enter the play not as playwright or director but metaphorically only, as manipulators of the lives of others. A character of this kind is, one has the impression, much more common in drama than in the novel. The role of the master plotter is already in Greek tragedy; Dionysus in *The Bacchae* is an obvious example. I note in passing that the word 'plot' and the French and Italian equivalents, *intrigue* and *trama*, are used of both sinister plans in real life and the complication and dénouement of plays. At least twelve of Shakespeare's plays, a third of the whole, have characters who control the movements of others: for example, the diabolic Iago, Prospero the magician, and the Haroun-al-Rashid-like Duke in *Measure for Measure*. Ben Jonson's Volpone glories more in the cunning purchase of his wealth (the way he and Mosca 'play' their victims) than in the glad possession. Other instances may be found in Molière, Ibsen, Shaw, Anouilh and T. S. Eliot. Even the single figure in Beckett's *Krapp's Last Tape* exercises despotic control over the appearances of his earlier selves and so may very clearly be seen as an internalization of the playwright.

By internalizing his own function as a maker of plots or the director's function as *metteur en scène*, by creating, for example, an Iago who, like himself, organizes in advance and orchestrates the movements and responses of the other characters, Shakespeare creates a series of ironic situations. The audience, who has been given early notice of Iago's real character, see Othello, Cassio and Desdemona all blindly confiding in, trusting in, and following the advice of honest Iago. The irony is not less powerful for being formally simple:

for while this honest fool [Cassio]
Plies Desdemona to repair his fortunes,
And she for him pleads strongly to the Moor,
I'll pour this pestilence into his ear,
That she repeals him for her body's lust;
And by how much she strives to do him good,
She shall undo her credit with the Moor;
So will I turn her virtue into pitch,
And out of her own goodness make the net
That shall enmesh 'em all.

(II, iii, 342–51)

THE SCRIPT

The novel, in its conventional pretence to be history, assumes that *first* things happen and *then* they are recorded. Diderot, however, in his *Jacques le fataliste*, reverses this, presenting the reader with the doctrine of determinism in terms of divine authorship: 'Tout ce qui nous arrive de bien et de mal ici-bas était écrit là-haut.' This corresponds to a reality of the theatre where everything that happens to the dramatis personae, good or bad, has already been written down by the playwright; it is his script, supplemented by the director's instructions, that determines the action of the play for the actors. But the dramatic pretence is that the action is taking place now in an undetermined temporal sequence and this is so even with history plays set in an unalterable past.

There is thus a potentially ironic contradiction between the script, in the sense of a 'prescript' or setting down of what must take place, and the representation of a seemingly undetermined 'taking place'. This irony is actualized with the metaphorical internalization of the script as a sense of destiny or unavoidable fate, embodied sometimes only as a feeling:

my mind misgives
Some consequence, yet hanging in the stars,

Shall bitterly begin his fearful date
With this night's revels.

(*Romeo and Juliet*, I, iv, 105–9)

and sometimes more concretely as an oracle, a dream, a curse or a prophecy. The most elaborate example in Shakespeare is the old Queen Margaret's wide-ranging prophetic curse in *King Richard III* which functions as a supplementary structural device, the audience being reminded of it as one after another of the characters falls from high place. Here as elsewhere the irony lies in the characters' explicit refusal to take the curse seriously. The fact that the reception of drama must keep pace with the performance, added to the tightness of construction of tragedies on the classical model, no doubt helps to create a sense of an inevitable working out of events. In comedies chance and surprise tend to play a larger part in contrast to the destiny and suspense of tragedy.

THE ACTOR

The kinds of irony I have associated with the internalizations of playwright (or director) and script resemble each other in being based on a character's ignorance of what is going to happen. The kind of irony that can be associated with the internalization of the actor differs from these in being based on a character's ignorance of his or another's nature or identity. This kind of irony is certainly no less frequent nor any less deeply rooted in the nature of theatre and drama than the ironies of plot and fate.

To act is not only to engage in an action, it is also to impersonate, and this is a matter of both personal identity and physical disguise. We can regard a character as an internalized actor if what he does and how he is regarded within the play is analogous to what an actor does and how he is regarded in respect of the play. There is hardly a play in which there is not a hidden identity, literal or metaphorical, accidental or deliberate, that eventually comes to light: someone gives himself a new name or the name of another;

with the help of mask, costume, accent or mannerism he pretends not to be himself or to be someone else; without intending it, he is mistaken for another or for a stranger; he does not know his parentage or mistakenly thinks he does; or what is hidden or mistaken is not his identity but his moral character or his motives. In the end he unmasks himself or is unmasked, recovers the secret of his birth, is stripped of his pretences or finds his lost twin. When the play is over, the actor resumes his own identity, his real name and his street clothes.

Drama is built upon two great questions, 'What is going to happen?' and 'Who is this?' There is, in fact, a play called *Who?* (by the Australian dramatist Jack Hibberd) and another called *Identité* (by Robert Pinget). Identity, and the questions and affirmations it involves, might almost be the major theme of drama from Oedipus' tragic self-discovery to Pirandello's *Maschere Nude* and beyond. Shakespeare alone could provide a hundred instances, from the famous opening words of *Hamlet* – 'Who's there?' 'Nay, answer me. Stand and unfold yourself' – to Lear's anguished question, 'Who is it that can tell me who I am?' or Troilus' dilemma, 'This is, and is not, Cressid' or Othello's deliberately ironic 'mistake' when he hears Desdemona deny her guilt:

> I cry you mercy then.
> I took you for that cunning whore of Venice
> That married with Othello.

> (IV, ii, 89–91)

The internalization of costume, of an actor's dressing up as someone and later re-assuming his own clothes, is also frequent in drama. There is actual disguising; half a dozen of Shakespeare's boy-actors acting girls' parts actualize the potential irony by dressing themselves up as boys. There is also metaphorical dressing up; Prince Hal's first words in his new role of king are,

> This new and gorgeous garment, majesty,
> Sits not so easy on me as you think.

> (*King Henry IV, Part 2*, V, ii, 44–5)

And at the end of Macbeth's career we are told,

> now does he feel his title
> Hang loose about him, like a giant's robe
> Upon a dwarfish thief.
>
> (V, ii, 20–2)

King Lear in the storm recognizes that his majesty is no more the real man than the costume lent for an actor's role is the actor. He begins to strip: 'Off, off, you lendings!' Physical stripping may be as good theatre in high tragedy as in low night-club. Robert Pinget's *Abel et Bela* begins by asking 'What exactly is theatre?' Several answers are proposed only to be rejected until the finale shows that 'the essential, universal, human heart of theatre is – the spectacle of men and women undressing'. This, if we took it literally, would not be a serious answer, but we are surely meant to take it metaphorically. Moral exposure is undeniably good theatre: witness the deflation of the *miles gloriosus* of Roman comedy and all the stripping and self-stripping in such plays as *Who's Afraid of Virginia Woolf?*. In *Le Balcon*, Jean Genet exemplifies nearly every possible variant of both the identity and the disguise themes.

The ironies made possible when a character is mistaken as to his own or another's identity or character are mostly too obvious to need spelling out. The simplest form is perhaps when a character present in disguise hears himself referred to in the third person:

GENTLEMAN. They say Edgar . . . is with the Earl of Kent in Germany.
KENT. Report is changeable.

(*King Lear*, IV, vii, 91–3)

The irony may be equally straightforward when it is a character's moral nature that is mistaken; Iago is accepted in the role he plays of the plain, honest soldier. But an irony of this sort can be presented subtly:

DUNCAN.   There's no art
To find the mind's construction in the face:
He [Cawdor] was a gentleman on whom I built
An absolute trust—
            (*Enter* MACBETH, BANQUO, ROSSE and ANGUS.)
                        O worthiest cousin!
                                    (*Macbeth*, I, iv, 11–14)

I have already spoken in general terms of the potentially ironic disparity between a character's self-definition and the definition of him constructed by the play itself. It is sometimes quite clear that a character is producing himself not as he is but as he would like to think he is. I mentioned Malvolio and Brutus and could have mentioned Mrs Malaprop and Polonius (and all those vain and pompous fools made in similar moulds), Hjalmar Ekdal in *The Wild Duck*, Alceste in *Le Misanthrope*, and Richard II:

I had forgot myself, am I not king?
Awake, thou coward majesty! thou sleepest.
Is not the king's name twenty thousand names?
Arm, arm, my name! a puny subject strikes
At thy great glory. Look not to the ground,
Ye favourites of a king, are we not high?
High be our thoughts. I know my uncle York
Hath power enough to serve our turn.

                                    (III, ii, 83–90)

The irony is less clear cut when the character plays a part that is variable or unclear, as when Hamlet puts on an antic disposition. It becomes complex when uncertainty as to who or what one is spills over from one level of illusion to another, as in Molière's *Impromptu de Versailles*, where there is a dispute among the actors whether '*le marquis*' is the actor playing the part of the marquis or the real person that the marquis is supposed to represent, or as in those plays of Pirandello's that call into question the conventional distinctions between reality and appearance, face and mask, identity and role.

THE AUDIENCE

The internalization of the audience is less frequent but by no means uncommon. I am not thinking here of the less usual case of characters in a play forming the audience of a rehearsal or a play-within-a-play. (When, as in *The Knight of the Burning Pestle*, such an audience insists on making changes in the play, what we have is Romantic Irony.) I have in mind the much simpler phenomenon of 'discrepant awareness'. Just as the audience generally knows more than the characters, so one or more characters may be shown as also having or acquiring a similar superiority relative to the other characters. When Electra, in Sophocles' play, finds out that her brother, supposedly dead, has returned she knows what the audience has known from the beginning and, of course, by keeping the secret maintains the superior situation of an observer. In comedy the exemplary case perhaps is the concealed rather than the reticent observer. In Racine, the situation of Britannicus, not knowing that Nero, from a concealed position, is listening to his conversation with Junie and of Junie, forced to watch Britannicus endangering himself but unable to tell him why she can only say what will upset him, is a situation repeated in essential in a hundred bedroom farces. It is highly instructive that the propriety of this famous scene was criticized on the grounds that it was '*une situation de comédie*'. It is, in fact, *une situation d'ironie*.

Dramatic Irony appears whenever the audience sees a character confidently unaware of his ignorance. It becomes more powerful when the discrepant awareness exists within the play and not just in the theatre. We, the audience, know from the beginning who Oedipus is and upon whom he has called down a curse. But how much more terrible is the irony of his continuing ignorance when we see one character after another coming to share our knowledge! The variety and the power of Dramatic Irony depend on other factors as well: whether or not the language spoken by or heard by the victim of the irony has, unknown to him, a double reference to the real situation and the situation as he sees it; whether there are concealed characters and whether these are victims or observers; and what the relationship is between the characters. The following from Euripides' *Iphigenia in Aulis* is powerful enough to stand up to a plain translation from a difficult text. Iphigenia thinks she has been brought to Aulis to be married to Achilles; her father, Agamemnon, cannot bring himself to tell her that at his command she has been brought there to be sacrificed:

> IPHIGENIA. Father, O I am glad to see you after this long time.
>
> AGAMEMNON. Yes, and your father to see you. What you say holds true for both of us.
>
> IPHIGENIA. You did well to have me brought to you, Father.
>
> AGAMEMNON. That is something, child, I cannot confirm or deny.
>
> IPHIGENIA. What is it? You looked troubled, for all your gladness seeing me.
>
> AGAMEMNON. A man has many worries when he is a king and a general.   (640–5)
>
> IPHIGENIA. You are going on a long journey, Father, leaving me behind.
>
> AGAMEMNON. It is the same for both of us, daughter.
>
> IPHIGENIA. Ah! If only it were right for me to sail with you!
>
> AGAMEMNON. You have a voyage to make too and you will not forget your father there.
>
> IPHIGENIA. Will I sail with my mother, or alone?
>
> AGAMEMNON. Alone, separated from father and mother.
>
> IPHIGENIA. You are sending me away to a new home somewhere, aren't you, Father?
>
> AGAMEMNON. That is enough. Girls should not know such things.
>
> IPHIGENIA. Please hurry back from Phrygia, Father, after victory there.

AGAMEMNON. First I must offer sacrifice here.

IPHIGENIA. Yes, we must look to the proper performance of our duty to the gods at any rate.

AGAMEMNON. You will see, for you will stand near the lustral bowl.

IPHIGENIA. Then, I will lead the dance round the altar, Father.

(664–76)

A recent work, Thomas Van Laan's *Role-Playing in Shakespeare* (Toronto, 1978) lists some seventy earlier books and articles on such topics in Shakespeare (and others) as theatrical imagery, the world-as-theatre metaphor, the play-within-the-play, the character as playwright, director, scenarist, actor or role-player, and the disguise and identity themes. Most of these post-date two influential works, Anne Righter's *Shakespeare and the Idea of the Play* (London, 1962) and Lionel Abel's *Metatheatre: A New View of Dramatic Form* (New York, 1963). The former, among other things, exhibits the extent of the theatrical self-consciousness of Shakespeare's plays; the latter has as its subject a form of drama (metatheatre) defined as 'theatre pieces about life seen as already theatricalized' and as 'the necessary form for dramatizing characters who, having full self-consciousness, cannot but participate in their own dramatization' (pp. 60, 78). So there is nothing very original in my more general hypothesis that plays tend naturally to internalize their immediate theatrical context and by doing so actualize the ironies that are latent in playmaking itself, seen as the creation of a mock-world by and within the real world of writing, producing, acting and theatre-going.

Internalizations of one kind of another are found as early as drama itself: the internal dramatist as manipulating character (Dionysus in *The Bacchae*, Odysseus in *Philoctetes*), the actor as impersonating character (Orestes in the *Choephoroe*, Dionysus in *The Frogs*), the audience as character with superior knowledge (Neoptolemus in *Philoctetes*) and the script as oracle (*The Knights* of Aristophanes, *Oedipus Rex*); in the parodies of Euripides in Aristophanes' *Thesmophoriazusae* there is even, though it is very sketchy, a play-within-a-play. It cannot therefore be argued that the theatricalization of drama is a result of the heightened self-consciousness of the Renaissance and post-Renaissance, though this will have increased the incidence of internalization. The now familiar argument that man is a role-playing, game-playing animal likewise has only limited force since it could explain only one aspect of internalization.

Two other explanations offer themselves. One is that the theatre finds its way into plays because the theatre is what playwrights know about and authors generally deal with the world they know. In building his play a dramatist must think in terms of production and reception and often in terms of particular companies, actors, audiences and theatres (with their limitations and advantages of staging, lighting, sets and acoustics). All this will be present to his consciousness and may in part explain the frequency with which Shakespeare, for example, employs metaphorically such words as theatre, stage, pageant, show, play, tragedy, act, scene, prologue, player, auditor, applause and so on.

To this argument, based on the inescapable physical presence of the theatre and its consequent pressure upon the playwright's consciousness, we can add another, namely that what I have called the theatrical context of plays is itself potentially dramatic in the popular senses of 'exciting' and 'emotionally powerful', and consequently that playwrights will tend to enhance their plays by actualizing and incorporating this potential. The 'drama' of theatre is inherent in the stage itself, or any empty space accepted as a stage, as a place where something is about to happen. We wait for what is going to appear in a mood of expectation qualitatively different from anything we experience in the cinema or when we sit down to a novel. Stoppard in *Rosencrantz and Guildenstern are Dead* continually creates drama by suggesting that the real play is only now about to begin. He also draws attention to the unseen off-stage area as the source of future action:

ROSENCRANTZ. (*leaps up again, stamps his foot and shouts into the wings.*) All right, we know you're in there! Come out talking!

(p. 53)

The physical presence of even a single flesh and blood actor already gives a play an emotional dimension since an audience cannot help responding in one way or another. The presence of two actors sets up different expectations of interaction and conflict depending on such things as distance, posture, age and sex. The fact of impersonation, someone dressed up as and behaving as if he were someone else, is also inherently dramatic; something of what an actor feels when playing a role must be transmitted to the audience. The audience, for its part, has something like the special 'voyeuristic' feeling of the unobserved observer and generally also the pleasurable feeling of knowing more about the action being played out than those directly involved. Finally, there is the intensification of life that accompanies the exercise of imagination when actors and audience co-operate to create the dramatic illusion. All these things combine to make the theatre in itself dramatic, and this 'drama' a playwright can double either intuitively or, like Stoppard, very consciously by the processes of internalization and the consequent ironies I have discussed.

Irony in fiction

There are innumerable instances of irony in fiction that are not especially characteristic of any fictional genre. Tom Driscoll in *Pudd'nhead Wilson* asks Wilson 'cheerily and good-naturedly', 'Well, how does the law come on? Had a case yet?' Obviously this sort of remark, ironic since he knows Wilson has been a total failure as a lawyer, might equally well be found in a play or heard in the street. Later, at the very moment of Wilson's discovering that Tom is a murderer, he (Tom) as yet ignorant that he has betrayed himself, passes another ironical remark, 'Don't take it so hard; a body can't win every time; you'll hang someone yet.' This situation is as much Dramatic Irony as Clytemnestra's mocking of Electra, 'You and Orestes – will you not silence me?' Fielding, who was a dramatist before he turned to the novel, gives us in *Tom Jones* scene after scene of ironies that would be as much as home in the theatre as in the novel, though none perhaps as theatrical as that where Jones hides his Sophia's maid behind the curtains when Lady Bellaston unexpectedly arrives (Book XV, Chapter 7). She is at first astonished by Jones' failure to respond to her amorous provocations, while Jones in turn is conscious of being 'in one of the most disagreeable and distress'd Situations imaginable'. 'Nothing', Fielding comments, 'can be imagined more comic, nor yet more tragical than this Scene would have been, if it had lasted much longer.'

The Irony of Events too, is common enough in prose fiction. In O. Henry's 'Gift of the Magi' (*Complete Works of O. Henry*, New York, 1953) a young man sells his watch to buy combs for his wife's long hair which she has sold to buy him a watchchain. But it is not more typical of fiction than of drama whether on a small or large scale; a story of confidence overthrown or of suspicions revealed as baseless may be as 'naturally' enacted as narrated. Perhaps it is more natural to drama than to the novel because the relative absence of detail in drama makes for a cleaner and clearer structural line and a sharper contrast between what is hoped or feared and what actually happens. What Lukács says in *The Historical Novel* (Harmondsworth, 1962) shows him to be thinking of the novel as exhibiting an ironic reversal on the scale of its overall structure: 'the hero [of *Wilhelm Meister*] realizes that he has achieved something quite different from what he set out to achieve.' But however true it may be that, as he says, 'the force of social circumstances proves stronger than the intentions of the hero and emerges triumphant from the struggle', one can still say that this kind of 'structural' irony is more visible and immediate in drama where the 'unstoppability' of the performance and the dynamic thrust towards the imminent, the 'about to happen', reinforce the causal dependence of events. In Goethe's *Wilhelm Meister* as contrasted with *Volpone* the ironic structure becomes apparent only on reflection.

More typical of the novel is what I have called Self-betraying Irony. Carson McCullers' Portia rebukes Mick for expressing revengefulness: 'That ain't no Christian way to talk.' But she is totally unaware of revealing the dubious Christianity of her own sentiments when she adds 'Us can just rest back and know they going to be chopped up with pitch-forks and fried everlasting by Satan.' This kind of irony is commonly revealed through speech, and so one is not surprised to find it in Plato's dialogues, in Browning's dramatic monologues (and Burns' 'Holy Willie's Prayer') and generally in plays; in the last section I mentioned a number of characters in plays, and not all were overtly comic characters, who produced themselves according to a mistaken self-image but at the same time by word or act inadvertently revealed their true nature.

This kind of irony, where the false image a character has formed of himself clashes with the image that the work enables the reader to form, is common in novels. Jane Austen opens *Persuasion*:

> Sir Walter Elliot, of Kellynch-hall, in Somersetshire, was a man who, for his own amusement, never took up any book but the Baronetage; there he found occupation for an idle hour, and consolation in a distressed one; there his faculties were roused into admiration and respect, by contemplating the limited remnant of the earliest patents; there any unwelcome sensations, arising from domestic affairs, changed naturally into pity and contempt, as he turned over the almost endless creations of the last century – and there, if every other leaf were powerless, he could read his own history with an interest which never failed – this was the page at which the favourite volume always opened: 'ELLIOT OF KELLYNCH-HALL'.

An irony of this kind, however, we can see to be only a sub-class of a wider irony where the false image a character has formed of the world he inhabits clashes with the real world. This wider irony, including its not always easily distinguishable sub-class, has been from the beginning a staple irony of the novel. From *Don Quixote* (1605) to the present there has been an unbroken line of novels, tragic, comic or satiric, in which the hero or some lesser victim has vainly attempted (vainly from the reader's point of view, however successfully from his own) to impose unity upon the world by interpreting it in terms of his fears or wishes, theories or ideals, his own or those of his class. *Don Quixote* lives, as we say, in a world of his own in which the giants, princesses, armies and castles of chivalric romance have replaced the windmills, serving wenches, flocks of sheep and inns of contemporary Spain:

> The officer, not disposed to bear this language from one of so scurvy an aspect, lifted up his lamp, and dashed it, with all its contents, at the head of Don Quixote, and then made his retreat in the dark. 'Surely', quoth Sancho Panza, 'this must be the enchanted Moor; and he reserves the treasure for others, and for us only fisty-cuffs and lamp-shots.' 'It is even so', answered Don Quixote; 'and it is to no purpose to regard these affairs of enchantments, or to be out of humour or angry with them; for, being invisible, and mere phantoms, all endeavours to seek revenge would be fruitless. Rise, Sancho, if thou canst, and call the governor of this fortress, and procure me some oil, wine, salt, and rosemary, to make the healing balsam; for in truth I want it much at this time, as the wound this phantom has given me bleeds very fast.'
>
> (Trans. Charles Jarvis, Book I, Chapter 17)

Pangloss in *Candide* is the Don Quixote of Leibnizian philosophical optimism and as such is able to interpret every disaster as both necessary and beneficial. Candide wonders whether syphilis is not of diabolic origin:

> – Not at all, replied that great man; it's an indispensable part of the best of worlds, a necessary ingredient; if Columbus had not

caught, on an American island, this sickness which attacks the source of generation and sometimes prevents generation entirely – which thus strikes at and defeats the greatest end of Nature herself – we should have neither chocolate nor cochineal.

(Trans. and ed. Robert M. Adams, New York, 1968, p. 8)

Gradgrind in *Hard Times* is the Don Quixote of a debased Benthamite utilitarianism. The book opens:

'Now, what I want is, Facts. Teach these boys and girls nothing but Facts. Facts alone are wanted in life. Plant nothing else, and root out everything else. You can only form the minds of reasoning animals upon Facts: nothing else will ever be of any service to them. This is the principle on which I bring up my own children, and this is the principle on which I bring up these children. Stick to Facts, sir!'

Madame Bovary is the Don Quixote of sentimentalism:

Then she recalled the heroines of the books that she had read, and the lyric legion of these adulterous women began to sing in her memory with the voice of sisters that charmed her. She became herself, as it were, an actual part of these imaginings, and realised the love-dream of her youth as she saw herself in this type of amorous women whom she had so envied.

(Trans. E. Marx-Aveling, London, 1957, p. 134)

We enter here the realm of the day-dream, refuge of those whose actual circumstances do not do them justice. Christina Pontifex in *The Way of all Flesh* has reveries that can only be called operatic:

Christina said that the will was simply fraudulent, and was convinced that it could be upset if she and Theobald went the right way to work. Theobald, she said, should go before the Lord Chancellor, not in full court but in chambers, where he could explain the whole matter; or, perhaps it would be even better if she were to go herself – and I dare not trust myself to describe the reverie to which this last idea gave rise. I believe in the end Theobald died, and the Lord Chancellor (who had become a widower a few weeks earlier) made her an offer, which, however, she firmly but not ungratefully declined; she should ever, she said, continue to think of him as a friend – at this point the cook came in, saying the butcher had called, and what would she please to order.

(Chapter 37)

In the works from which these examples have been drawn the character's self-image or view of the world is variously revealed as false. Pangloss' impossible optimism, for example, is ironized primarily by what happens to him and his companions; the best of all possible worlds is shown to be full of diseases, brutality, vice, fraud, natural disasters, religion and war. Gradgrind's theory of education is ironized by what it leads to, the near destruction of the lives of his own children. From the beginning Dickens turns the reader against Gradgrind, by giving him such a name, by describing him as if he were a manufactured object – 'square forefinger . . . square wall of a forehead . . . square coat, square legs, square shoulders' and much more – and by giving this opening chapter an ironical title 'The one thing needful'. Jane Austen likewise exposes Sir Walter Elliot by his own stupid words and deeds, by the outcome of the story, by telling us directly that he is vain, and, more extensively than Dickens, by verbal irony. Of Sir Walter we are told that 'He considered the blessing of beauty as inferior only to the blessing of a baronetcy; and the Sir Walter Elliot, who united these gifts, was the constant object of his warmest respect and devotion' (Chapter 1).

Verbal Irony on the part of the narrator is more characteristic of eighteenth- and nineteenth-century novels than of those of this century. Since Flaubert and James, more and more novelists have come to believe that 'the art of fiction does not begin until the novelist thinks of his story as a matter to be *shown*, to be so exhibited that it will tell itself' (Percy Lubbock, *The Craft of Fiction*, London, 1921, p. 62. See Wayne C. Booth, *The Rhetoric of Fiction*, 1961, *passim*). Suppressing or impersonalizing the narrator has relieved us of the irritatingly intrusive writer with his 'dear reader' confidentiality but it has also made impossible, among other useful and desirable effects, the special kinds of novelistic irony best exemplified by Fielding but also to be found in Sterne, Jane Austen, Thackeray and George Eliot, and in Flaubert and James too. In Fielding's *Tom Jones* the ironic authorial dimension is of such major aesthetic importance that we might be justified in calling the work not so much a novel as a guided tour through a novel, a highly unusual one, the guide's words having equal value with what he is exhibiting.

> Indeed she was so far from regretting Want of Beauty, that she never mentioned that Perfection (if it can be called one) without Contempt; and would often thank God she was not as handsome as Miss such a one, whom perhaps Beauty had led into Errors, which she might have otherwise avoided. Miss *Bridget Allworthy* (for that was the Name of this Lady) very rightly conceived the Charms of Person in a Woman to be no better than Snares for herself, as well as for others; and yet so discreet was she in her Conduct, that her Prudence was as much on the Guard, as if she had all the Snares to apprehend which were ever laid for her whole Sex. Indeed, I have observed (tho' it may seem unaccountable to the Reader) that this Guard of Prudence, like the Trained Bands, is always readiest to go on Duty where there is the least Danger. It often basely and cowardly deserts those Paragons for whom the Men are all wishing, sighing, dying, and spreading every Net in their Power; and constantly attends at the Heels of that higher Order of Women, for whom the other Sex have a more distant and awful Respect, and whom (from Despair, I suppose, of Success) they never venture to attack.
>
> (Book I, Chapter 2)

This authorial method of ironizing a character is specifically novelistic; in a play one character may speak ironically of another but he can never speak with the absolute authority of the writer.

Other methods of exposing a character's false or inadequate view of himself or the world at large may also be found in plays, and here what is characteristic of novels is not the method but the choice of ironic object, the greater focus upon character and the inner life of characters. How is this to be explained? In the previous section I tried to show that the kinds of irony characteristic of drama were the result of the internalization of an inherent duality, theatre versus drama, the bringing into the play itself its immediate theatrical context (script, production, impersonation and audience). Can it now be shown that there is something in the nature of the novel that would favour the appearance of the kind of irony illustrated in the last few pages? I think that it can and that the brief answer is that the novel has developed over the last two or three centuries as the form best adapted for dealing with the inner life of men and women living in our complex modern society.

Perhaps the most significant thing one can say about prose fiction is that there is remarkably little one can say about it in general. No other form is so formless; or putting it another way, no form is so open to formal diversity in terms of length, chronological ordering of material, and mode of narration and evaluation, to mention only the most obvious elements. Even if we put aside the short story and the novella, conveniently forgetting the highly arbitrary nature of the generic division that enables us to do so, what can we say of the novel except that it is a relatively long fictional account of human thought and feeling, speech and action in a social setting? What else in common have *The Golden Ass* and *The Golden Bowl*, *Tristram Shandy* and *Treasure Island*, *The Last Days of Pompeii* and *Last Year in Marienbad*, *We* and *Watt*?

What is possibly of more importance is the fact that prose fiction, unlike drama, does not tie its audience, the individual reader, to a performance time. The reader's freedom to read at his own pace, to pause, to re-read and to reflect makes possible several things. It permits greater length, hence wider scope and finer detail, hence complexity, hence explanation, reflection and deliberation. It removes the need to hold the audience's attention by being on the one hand 'theatrical' and 'dramatic' and on the other hand immediately and easily intelligible. It permits instead events that are merely interesting and thought-provoking; Thomas Mann, in his 'The Art of the Novel' (*The Creative Vision*, ed. Haskell M. Block and Herman Salinger, 1960) quotes Schopenhauer as saying that the 'task of the novelist is not to narrate great events but to make small ones interesting'. All this points in one direction, to the novel as the form we turn to for the experience of understanding a subjectivized social existence.

The last three words are intended to suggest a duality of inner and outer life and hence scope for ironic observation. They will serve also to distinguish the novel from the single-visioned romance, whether the *roman d'aventures*, picaresque novel or thriller that confines itself mainly to the outer world, or the lyric romance of the inner life of an individual. Evidence for the historical changes that brought about a heightened awareness of the self and consequently a growing antithesis between inner and outer world may be found in lexicology (an enormous increase throughout the seventeenth century of compound words beginning with 'self-', including 'self-consciousness' itself), in religion (Everyman in the fifteenth-century morality play is saved by his Good Deeds; Christian in *Pilgrim's Progress* (1678) is supported or saved by his inner qualities, his companions Faithful and Hopeful), in philosophy (the switch since Descartes from ontology to epistemology, to the mind as the chief concern of philosophy or even as the sole reality), and in literary theory (Aristotle in his *Poetics* clearly subordinated character to action, but Dryden in his *Essay of Dramatic Poesy* as clearly thought what happens and what is done to be less central than the characters' reactions thereto: 'the audience . . . watch the movements of their minds, as much as the changes of their fortunes. For the imaging of the first is properly the work of a poet; the latter he borrows from the historian').

To this increased turning inwards there was added the complementary growth of the concept of the outer world as over-complex, dehumanized and alienating: instead of the city the metropolis, instead of the local market the global market forces, instead of the squire and the king the machinery of bureaucracy and the adding up of votes, instead of the workshop the mass-produced component, instead of God's purposes the 'big bang' theory and the second law of thermodynamics.

Either development provides scope for irony. The ironic novelist can on the one hand 'romanticize' the inner life of his characters and on the other 'banalize' their social context. So Christina Pontifex's extravagant reverie of marrying the Lord Chancellor is cut short by the need to order the meat; Butler here shows that he understood the principle of high contrast. The incident is, of course, symptomatic of Christina Pontifex's general inability to emerge from the cocoon of her middle-class Anglican upbringing and see the world in any but the most subjective terms. Not that the world of butchers and barbers, windmills and cotton mills, represents any absolute reality. In fact, what Dickens' *Hard Times* argues is that Gradgrind's 'objectivity', his rejection of fancy, is itself a false and dangerous illusion, vulnerable to irony as the dreams of Christina or Emma Bovary.

The theory of the novel of the early Lukács becomes relevant at this point. For Lukács the world of the Homeric epic was a totality that pre-dated the division into inner and outer worlds. This totality, once 'given', now exists only as the object of a quest, as an ideal, that of reintegrating subjectivity and objectivity, of bringing together in a new way what history has been driving further apart, namely an alienated private life and a meaningless alienating public life, the one becoming impoverished as the other disintegrates. This viewpoint enables us to see *Don Quixote* as much more than the story of a man whose excessive reading of chivalrous romances has made him crazy to the point of mistaking inns for castles and becoming thereby the butt of Cervantes' ironic mockery. What Lukács shows us is something more interesting, Cervantes' awareness, acquired at first hand, of a world that is already alienating:

The first great novel of world literature stands at the beginning of the time when the Christian God began to forsake the world; when man became lonely and could find meaning and substance only in his own soul, whose home was nowhere; when the world, released from its paradoxical anchorage in a beyond that is truly present, was abandoned to its immanent meaninglessness . . . . Cervantes lived in the period of the last, great and desperate mysticism, the period of a fanatical attempt to renew the dying religion from within; . . . a period of great confusion of values in the midst of an as yet unchanged value system. And Cervantes, the faithful Christian and naïvely loyal patriot, creatively exposed the deepest essence of this demonic problematic: the purest heroism is bound to become grotesque, the strongest faith is bound to become madness, when the ways leading to the transcendental home have become impassable; reality does not have to correspond to subjective evidence, however genuine and heroic.

(The Theory of the Novel, trans. Anna Bostock,
London, 1971, pp. 103–4)

This view renders the irony not only more sombre but also more complex since we can see it as directed against 'the prosaic vulgarity of outward life' as well as against a hero left behind by history and unable to comprehend the new form social life was taking.

For Lukács, any Western novel that truly reflects its social context will necessarily be a story of dissonance, breakdown or failure, inner and outer life having become totally at odds with one another. The hero cannot accomplish his inner urge to make sense of his world or establish his identity, any success that he may have (Lukács cites Pontoppidan's *Hans im Glück*) proving illusory or inadequate. Hence the essentially ironigenic nature of the novel. But to say that the novelist can see and present to his readers the irony of his hero's inevitable failure is to imply only his understanding of the problem not its abolition; there is still the further step of seeing his own work in the same light, as being itself an attempt to make sense of the world and so equally open to irony.

We should be reminded at this point of the Romantic Irony of
Friedrich Schlegel and Karl Solger, and in fact Lukács refers to
their concept of irony as 'the self-recognition and, with it, self-
abolition of subjectivity' (ibid., p. 74). The novelist's ironic recognition of his own ironic predicament though melancholy is not as
black as would be a non-ironic surrender, Lukács explains:

> Whilst irony depicts reality as victorious, it reveals not only that
> reality is as nothing in the face of its defeated opponent, not only
> that the victory of reality can never be a final one, that it will
> always, again and again, be challenged by new rebellions of the
> idea, but also that reality owes its advantage not so much to its
> own strength, which is too crude and directionless to maintain
> the advantage, as to the inner (although necessary) problematic
> of the soul weighted down by its ideals.

(ibid., p. 86)

Or more poetically:

> Irony gives form to the malicious satisfaction of God the creator
> at the failure of man's weak rebellions against his mighty, yet
> worthless creation and, at the same time, to the inexpressible
> suffering of God the redeemer at his inability to re-enter that
> world. Irony, the self-surmounting of a subjectivity that has
> gone as far as it was possible to go, is the highest freedom that
> can be achieved in a world without God. That is why it is not
> only the sole possible *a priori* condition for a true, totality-
> creating objectivity but also why it makes that totality – the
> novel – the representative art-form of our age.

(ibid., pp. 92–3)

The irony that Lukács sees as the 'normative mentality of the
novel' is Romantic Irony. As we saw in chapter 2 Romantic Irony,
as an artistic programme, envisages a double aim: by incorporating
the artist's self-awareness to imbue the created work (which as
such can only be limited and partial) with the dynamic of the
creative process, and simultaneously but in reverse, to invent a

form for expressing this artistic illusion of self-creativity. A successful work in the Romantic Irony mode will seem to be art raised to a higher power, a work whose raw material was already art. It will have the freshness of spontaneity and the urbanity of total artistic control. It will generate the paradoxical feeling of an enclosed infinity as in '*mise en abîme*' pictures (the figure on the Quaker Oats packet is depicted as holding up a packet of Quaker Oats on which he is depicted, etc.) or as in the opposed mirrors in one of the rooms in the Schönbrunn in Vienna or a feeling of infinite dialectic as in those drawings that appear now as a solid cube, now as a hollow box. As Friedrich Schlegel says in a notebook fragment,

> Complete submergence in either feeling [*Sentimentalität*] or inventiveness [*Fantasie*] may lead to Romanticism of a sort, but only with the highest degree of both will there be created that tension of opposites which is absolute Romanticism or Romantic Irony.
>
> (*Friedrich Schlegel: Literary Notebooks, 1797–1801*, ed. Hans Eichner, Toronto, 1957, p. 84)

In my view the clearest, perhaps because most consciously exemplary, examples of Romantic Irony are to be found not in the Romantic period but in the early twentieth century in the novels of Thomas Mann, a contemporary of Lukács and the subject of one of his studies. Thomas Mann was a conscientious student of literature and literary studies and as such no stranger to Schlegel's theory of Romantic Irony. In fact he himself once said of 'the problem of irony' that it was 'without exception the profoundest and most fascinating in the world' ('Goethe and Tolstoy', *Essays of Three Decades*, trans. H. T. Lowe-Porter, London, 1947, p. 122). Almost any of his major works might be chosen to exemplify Romantic Irony, but I shall restrict myself to his *Doctor Faustus* (1947).

In planning this novel, Thomas Mann sets his sights very high. But as a true Schlegelian he knew that one cannot seriously propose to achieve greatness without immediately introducing a false note. The solution was not to attempt less but deliberately and audaciously to write the false note into the work – in the person of a narrator who would be a parody of Thomas Mann himself, cultured, highly-educated and well-intentioned but old-fashioned, earnest, even somewhat pompous and hence ridiculous. This ironized narrator, Zeitblom, would function as a lightning-rod; he would attract and absorb whatever hubris there was in the work's intentions and Thomas Mann could safely be as ambitious as he liked.

As the title indicates, the novel is a modern version of the sixteenth-century Faust legend, one more in a series of modernizations that includes Goethe's play. Hence it is inescapably a 'literary' work. At the same time it pretends not to be literature but biography, 'The life of the German composer Adrian Leverkühn, as told by a friend.' All the same, the biography has scarcely begun when Zeitblom discovers that effectively to relate actualities he must obey the rules of art and (as Schlegel says) not blurt out everything at once but practise self-limitation. But then to shape one's work and so become a creative artist implies the need to distance oneself from one's subject, and this is a wanton betrayal of one's real feelings.

In short, art is both necessary and inadequate for a true rendering of life. This truth which we find expressed in the opening chapter is one of the principal themes of the whole work. The life of the composer, Adrian Leverkühn, is the record of a search for a way of breaking out of a musical impasse. What is a musical genius to do when he can 'see through' and master without effort every device and effect of music to the point where any piece of music, however lovely, seems like its own parody? This is not just a problem for music, and *Doctor Faustus* is not just the life of a musician (incorporating the history of Western music from the invention of polyphony through harmonic subjectivity and the sophisticated self-consciousness of musical parody to a second-order naïvety) but a work which, polyphonically, interweaves a

conspectus and definition of Germanness, culturally and politically conceived, and both exemplifies and discusses the problem-
atics of modern art. But if on one level art and life are shown as
having parted company, on another they are identified. Not only
does the hero represent Germany – collapsing into madness in
1930 along with the collapse of the Weimar republic – but both
modern music and modern Germany faced an imperative need to
break out or break through into a radically new world.

Just as Thomas Mann ironically sets up the barrier state of a
fictional narrator to distance himself from the risks of taking his art
too seriously so, with equal irony, he protects himself against the
contrary charge that art has become a game, an irrelevance, a lie,
by making this charge a main theme of his novel and by turning his
fiction into history and documentation. More than one episode in
his hero's life is taken over from the life of Nietzsche, almost every
other character has a model in real life, and even a suicide note
written by Thomas Mann's sister is reproduced verbatim. He confesses to being, like Joyce, unable to admit, in matters of style,
anything but parody, which in so far as it is a refunctioning of
something which already exists has an element of the authentic.
Invention, as far as possible, is reduced to montage, the arrange-
ment of things not invented. But Mann is not like the author of *In
Cold Blood*; he does not write 'faction', for that is to abandon the
ironic dialectic of fact and fiction, necessity and freedom. This is
another theme in *Doctor Faustus* just as it was a strand in
Schlegel's theory of Romantic Irony.

I have touched only lightly on this infinitely elaborate novel
but perhaps have said enough to show that Thomas Mann's
'solution' to what he saw as the twentieth-century version of the
impossibility of reconciling subjectivity and objectivity, feeling
and form, art and life was in effect the 'solution' put forward
though more optimistically by Friedrich Schlegel, namely, to
recognize and even foreground within the work itself the necessary limitations of both art and artist, to recover the spontaneity
of naïve creativity by transforming earnest endeavour to ironic

playfulness, and to achieve both openness and an appearance of objectivity by

> that irony which glances at both sides, which plays slyly and irresponsibly – yet not without benevolence – among opposites, and is in no great haste to take sides and come to decisions; guided as it is by the surmise that in great matters, in matters of humanity, every decision may prove premature; that the real goal to reach is not decision, but harmony, accord. And harmony, in a matter of eternal contraries, may lie in infinity.
> ('Goethe and Tolstoy', op. cit., 1947, p. 173)

The harmony that lies in infinity is rather like the angle subtended at the meeting of parallel lines, and one suspects that Mann himself was ironically hinting at some such resemblance. All the same, his ironic stance is in the last analysis Apollonian or, as Kierkegaard would say, that of a 'mastered irony' having behind it the weight and authority of Mann's distinct temperament.

At the end of chapter 2 I quoted Roland Barthes praising Flaubert for his wielding of 'an irony fraught with uncertainty . . . so that one never knows whether he is responsible for what he writes (whether there is an individual subject behind his language)'. This separating out of writing as something independent of communication is now becoming widespread. In so far as it amounts to a denial of both mimesis and the relevance of intentionality it may well have been, as I have heard it explained, a translation, on the part of the French intellectual left, of the *refus de pouvoir* and the distrust of authority and property of the French marxists into the terms of literary theory. Be that as it may, any such distinction between writing and communicating *ipso facto* rules out irony as I have defined it. I have taken being ironical to mean transmitting a literal message in such a way or in such a context as to challenge a response in the form of a correct interpretation of one's intent, the transliteral meaning. In brief (Instrumental) Irony is an act, not simply a significance. Of writing that is designed to prevent interpretation in terms of intent one could use the word 'irony' only, it seems, as a synonym for 'uncertainty', that is as a word without any additional content and therefore redundant.

The establishment in recent years in both France and America of Deconstructionist criticism based on a view of writing as, in the words of Jacques Derrida, 'a structure cut off from any absolute responsibility or from consciousness as ultimate authority' (Jonathan Culler, *Structuralist Poetics*, London, 1975, p. 132) will probably lead to a recognition of the decreased usefulness to literary criticism of the term 'irony'. It seems less likely that the usefulness of the term will delay the establishment of Deconstructionism or some related movement.

Bibliography

The number of works in English which deal exclusively with the nature, concept, or history of irony is not large even if we include articles. There are even fewer in French, though many more in German. The most recent extensive bibliographies are in Hans-Egon Hass (comp.), *Ironie als Literarische Phänomen*, Köln, 1973 and Wayne C. Booth, *A Rhetoric of Irony*, Chicago, 1974. The number of articles on irony in individual authors or works is legion.

General works in English including translations

Collins, A., *A Discourse Concerning Ridicule and Irony in Writing*, London, 1729.
'Its wide-ranging and exhaustive use of examples, the representative nature of its arguments, and the emphasis of its orientation make it a milestone in the history of general concern over irony.' (Knox)

Schlegel, F., *Friedrich Schlegel's* Lucinde *and the Fragments*, trans. Peter Firchow, Minneapolis, 1971.
The brief novel, *Lucinde* (1799) exemplifies Romantic Irony but imperfectly. Most of what Schlegel said about Romantic Irony is to be found scattered through the Fragments (1797–1800) and in the amusing essay 'On Incomprehensibility'.

Thirlwall, C., 'On the Irony of Sophocles' in *The Philological Museum*, Vol. II, 1833, and in *Remains, Literary and Theological*, ed. J. Stewart Perowne, Vol. III, London, 1878.
There is a substantial summary of the theoretical part of this

essay (essential for the history of the concept of irony) in Thompson, *The Dry Mock*.

Kierkegaard, S., *The Concept of Irony, with Constant Reference to Socrates*, 1841, trans. Lee M. Capel, London, 1966.

Rewarding for those who have some familiarity with the concepts of nineteenth-century German philosophy, difficult for those who have not.

Pirandello, L., *On Humor*, 1920, ed. and trans. Antonio Illiano and D. P. Testa, Chapel Hill, 1975.

Pirandello's 'humour' is close to irony, particularly to what might be called the general irony of inevitable self-deception.

Thompson, J. A. K., *Irony: An Historical Introduction*, London, 1926.

Deals only with Greek and Latin authors, including orators and historians.

Chevalier, H., *The Ironic Temper: Anatole France and his Time*, New York, 1932.

The second and sixth chapters discuss irony in general.

Sedgewick, G. G., *Of Irony, Especially in Drama*, 1935, 2nd edn, Toronto, 1948.

A valuable chapter on the history of the concept of irony, though misleading on Romantic Irony. Other chapters on 'Irony in Drama', 'The Clytemnestra plays' and *Othello*.

Mann, T., 'Die Kunst des Romans', 1939, trans. as 'The Art of The Novel' in *The Creative Vision*, ed. Haskell M. Block and Herman Salinger, New York, 1960.

On the relationship of irony and the 'epic' novel.

Worcester, D., *The Art of Satire*, Cambridge, Mass., 1940.

Chapter 4, 'Irony, the Ally of Comedy'; Chapter 5, 'Irony, the Ally of Tragedy'; Chapter 6, Section iv, 'Rebirth of Irony'; Section v, 'Sphinxes without Secrets'. An eminently readable work.

Thompson, A. R., *The Dry Mock, A Study of Irony in Drama*, Berkeley, 1948.

Attempts a coherent theory of irony, but defines irony too

104 *Irony and the Ironic*

exclusively. Principal ironists discussed: Tieck, Pirandello, Molière, Shaw, Aeschylus, Sophocles, Euripides and Ibsen. An important work.

Brooks, C., 'Irony and "Ironic" Poetry', *College English*, IX (1948), pp. 231–7, revised as 'Irony as a Principle of Structure' for *Literary Opinion in America*, ed. Morton Zabel, New York, 1951 (rev. edn), pp. 729–41. See also Brooks' *The Well-Wrought Urn*, London, 1949.

> An influential essay that extended (and weakened) the concept of irony. Criticized by R. S. Crane in 'The Critical Monism of Cleanth Brooks' in *Critics and Criticism*, ed. R. S. Crane, Chicago, 1952, pp. 83–107, and by William Righter in his *Logic and Criticism*, London, 1963.

Wellek, R., *A History of Modern Criticism 1750–1950; II: The Romantic Age*, London, 1955.

> Valuable for its account of the German theorists.

Frye, N., *Anatomy of Criticism*, Princeton, 1957.

> An attempt to relate irony to other kinds of writing and to define its place in the evolution of imaginative literature.

Gurewitch, M. L., *European Romantic Irony*, Ph.D. dissertation (1957), Ann Arbor, 1962.

> An interesting general introduction with discussions of Byron, Baudelaire, Büchner, Carlyle, Flaubert, Théophile Gautier, Heine, Leopardi, Alfred de Musset and Stendhal.

Watt, I., 'The Ironic Tradition in Augustan Prose from Swift to Johnson', in *Restoration and Augustan Prose*, Los Angeles, 1957[?].

> Some valuable observations on the relationship between irony and eighteenth-century prose.

Booth, W. C., *The Rhetoric of Fiction*, Chicago, 1961.

> An indispensable treatment of the dangers of irony in 'impersonal' and 'point-of-view' narrative methods.

Knox, N., *The Word IRONY and Its Context, 1500–1755*, Durham, N.C., 1961.

> A detailed, scholarly account of the development of the concept of irony within the period named.

Hutchens, E., *Irony in* Tom Jones, Alabama, 1965.
   Has an introductory chapter on the nature of irony and an interesting classification of types of Verbal Irony.

Hatfield, G. W., *Henry Fielding and the Language of Irony*, Chicago and London, 1968.
   Of wider interest than the title may suggest.

Glicksberg, C. I., *The Ironic Vision in Modern Literature*, The Hague, 1969.
   The first work to be devoted entirely to General Irony. Discusses a wide range of European writers but tends to make them look too much the same.

Muecke, D. C., *The Compass of Irony*, London, 1969, repr. 1980.
   Part I discusses the nature of irony and illustrates in some detail the principal kinds. Part II deals chiefly with General and Romantic Irony and attempts to relate the development of these to developments in the history of European thought.

States, B. O., *Irony and Drama: A Poetics*, Ithaca and London, 1971.
   On the ironic reversal as characteristic of dramatic structure. By a follower of Kenneth Burke. Many plays are dealt with.

Knox, N., 'Irony' in *Dictionary of the History of Ideas*, ed. Philip P. Wiener, New York, 1973, Vol. II, pp. 626–34; 'On the Classification of Ironies' in *Modern Philology*, 70 (August, 1972), pp. 53–62.

Booth, W. C., *A Rhetoric of Irony*, Chicago, 1974.
   A clear account of the problems and pleasures of interpreting irony.

Fussell, P., *The Great War and Modern Memory*, New York, 1975.
   On the growth of ironic awareness in the modern period.

Mellor, A. K., *English Romantic Irony*, Cambridge, Mass. and London, 1980.
   A very clear account of Romantic Irony in Chapter 1. Other chapters on Byron, Keats, Carlyle, Coleridge and Lewis Carroll break new ground.

General works in other languages

Jankélévitch, V., *L'Ironie, ou La Bonne Conscience*, 1936, 2nd (rev.) edn, Paris, 1950.

A brilliant, indeed a dazzling work at a very general level. Largely indebted to Kierkegaard. Reviewed by Wilson O. Clough, 'Irony: A French Approach', *Sewanee Review*, XLVII, 1939, pp. 175–83.

Allemann, B., *Ironie und Dichtung*, Pfullingen, 1956.

On irony in German literature from Schlegel to Musil.

Strohschneider-Kohrs, I., *Die romantische Ironie in Theorie und Gestaltung*, Tübingen, 1960, 2nd edn, 1977.

The definitive study of Romantic Irony.

Behler, E., *Klassische Ironie, romantische Ironie, tragische Ironie. Zum Ursprung dieser Begriffe*, Darmstadt, 1972.

Bourgeois, R., *L'Ironie romantique*, Grenoble, 1974.

An introductory chapter on Romantic Irony and chapters on French writers of the period, including Constant, Stendhal and Nerval.

Poétique, November, 1978. A special number on irony.

Index